Beyond Illusion

The Secret Power of Yogamaya

Table of Contents

Introduction 2
- **Definition of Yogamaya** 2
- **Purpose and significance of the book** 8
- **Overview of themes and concepts to be covered** 11

Chapter 1: Understanding Yogamaya 15
- **Historical and philosophical context** 15
  - Roots in Hindu scriptures 18
  - Comparison with similar concepts in other traditions 21
- **The duality of reality: Maya vs. Yogamaya** 25
- **The role of Yogamaya in spiritual evolution** 28

Chapter 2: The Nature of Illusion 31
- **Defining illusion in spiritual terms** 31
- **How perceptions shape our reality** 34
- **The impact of societal conditioning on individual beliefs** 38

Chapter 3: The Layers of Reality 41
- **The physical vs. metaphysical dimensions** 41
- **Exploring the layers of consciousness** 45
- **The interplay of the material and spiritual worlds** 48

Chapter 4: The Role of Divine Play (Lila) 51
- **Understanding Lila in the context of Yogamaya** 51
- **The purpose of divine play in the universe** 54
- **How Lila creates the illusion of separateness** 57

Chapter 5: Awakening from the Illusion 60
- **Signs of spiritual awakening** 60
- **Techniques for recognizing and transcending illusion** 64
- **The significance of self-inquiry and mindfulness** 67

Chapter 6: Harnessing the Power of Yogamaya 70

- Practical applications of Yogamaya in daily life 70
- Meditative practices for connecting with Yogamaya 73
- The art of manifestation and intention setting 77

Chapter 7: The Role of Grace and Surrender 80
- Understanding the concept of divine grace 80
- The importance of surrendering to the flow of life 83
- Case studies of transformative experiences through surrender 86

Chapter 8: Yogamaya in Relationships 89
- The dynamics of relationships through the lens of Yogamaya 89
- Navigating attachments and detachment 92
- Building conscious relationships based on awareness 95

Chapter 9: The Path to Liberation (Moksha) 98
- The ultimate goal: transcending illusion 99
- Steps towards achieving liberation 102
- The significance of community and support on the journey 105

Conclusion 108
- Recap of the key themes 108
- Encouragement for continued exploration of Yogamaya 110
- Final thoughts on living beyond illusion 112

Appendix 114
- Recommended readings and resources 114
- Guided meditations and exercises 117
- Glossary of terms related to Yogamaya and Hindu philosophy 120

Introduction

- Definition of Yogamaya

In the vast ocean of Vedic literature, where mythology, philosophy, and spirituality intertwine, the concept of *Yogamaya* stands out as one of the most profound and complex mysteries. To understand Yogamaya, one must venture deep into the cosmic play orchestrated by the divine, where illusion and reality coalesce, and where time, space, and consciousness merge into one grand, infinite expanse.

To begin, let us break down the word itself. *Yoga* signifies union, connection, or a transcendental state of harmony between the individual soul (*jiva*) and the Supreme Being (*Paramatma*). *Maya*, on the other hand, refers to illusion, the magical force that veils the true nature of reality. Combined, *Yogamaya* refers to the divine power that controls both the real and the illusory aspects of existence. It is not just a form of illusion; rather, it is the supreme power that facilitates divine acts, orchestrating the entire cosmos with precision, and leading beings either towards bondage or liberation depending on their spiritual evolution.

The Origins of Yogamaya: A Mythical Perspective

To truly appreciate Yogamaya, one must travel back to the early days of the cosmos, to the realms beyond ordinary comprehension, where the eternal dance of creation, preservation, and dissolution unfolds under the gaze of the Supreme Being—Lord Vishnu. Yogamaya is often regarded as the personal energy of Vishnu or Krishna, manifesting in various forms to serve the divine will.

One of the earliest and most vivid depictions of Yogamaya appears in the story of Lord Krishna's birth. In the ancient Indian text, the *Bhagavata Purana*, we learn of a tyrannical king named Kamsa, who, upon hearing a prophecy that his sister Devaki's eighth son would be the cause of his death, imprisons her and her husband, Vasudeva. To prevent his death, Kamsa resolves to kill each of Devaki's children at birth.

But when Devaki conceives her eighth child—none other than the Supreme Lord Krishna—the divine plan comes into play. It is here that Yogamaya is invoked. As Devaki prepares to give birth, Lord Vishnu instructs her husband, Vasudeva, to exchange the newborn Krishna with a baby girl born to Yashoda and Nanda in the neighboring village of Gokul.

This baby girl is none other than Yogamaya herself, born to Yashoda in the guise of a mortal child. When Kamsa learns of the birth, he attempts to kill the child, unaware that this girl is no ordinary infant. Yogamaya, demonstrating her divine nature, slips from Kamsa's grip, ascends to the heavens, and reveals her true form as the Goddess, declaring that the one who is destined to end Kamsa's reign is already alive. Thus, Yogamaya plays her role in the divine leela (play), acting as both protector and the wielder of illusion. She deceives Kamsa while ensuring that Krishna is safe and can fulfill his destiny.

The Dual Nature of Yogamaya: Illusion and Liberation

What makes Yogamaya unique is her dual nature. On the one hand, she is the force of illusion (*maya*) that binds the individual soul to the material world, leading people to believe in the permanence of their transient lives. On the other hand, she is the guiding force (*yoga*) that can liberate the soul from this illusion, allowing one to experience union with the divine.

In the *Bhagavad Gita*, Lord Krishna tells Arjuna, "My divine energy, Yogamaya, is very difficult to overcome. But those who surrender to Me can easily cross beyond it" (Gita 7.14). Here, Krishna highlights the twofold nature of Yogamaya. For those who are immersed in ignorance, attached to their material desires and bound by their ego, Yogamaya acts as a veil, obscuring their understanding of the true nature of existence. They see the world as separate from the divine and remain entangled in the endless cycle of birth, death, and rebirth (*samsara*).

However, for the spiritually inclined, those who seek liberation (*moksha*) and the ultimate truth, Yogamaya acts as a divine bridge, leading them towards enlightenment. Through devotion, knowledge, and spiritual discipline, the veil of illusion is gradually lifted, revealing the underlying unity of all things.

Yogamaya as the Cosmic Playwright

One of the most intriguing aspects of Yogamaya is her role as the director of the cosmic drama, or *leela*. In this context, she is the power behind the play of the universe, weaving together the threads of fate, karma, and destiny. She choreographs the actions of gods, demons, and humans alike, ensuring that the cosmic balance is maintained.

In many ways, Yogamaya is akin to a master puppeteer. She manipulates the strings of illusion, allowing beings to believe that they are in control of their lives, while in reality, they are merely actors in a grander narrative. But unlike a conventional puppeteer, Yogamaya also gives her creations the power of free will, allowing them to choose their paths and face the consequences of their actions. It is through this interplay of free will and divine orchestration that the universe functions, with Yogamaya ensuring that all beings, whether bound by illusion or striving for liberation, are playing their roles in the cosmic drama.

Yogamaya and Her Manifestations

Yogamaya is not a singular entity but manifests in numerous forms, each tailored to the needs of the divine play. Some of the most well-known manifestations of Yogamaya include:

1. **Durga**: Often identified with Yogamaya, Durga is the fierce, protective mother goddess who slays demons and restores cosmic balance. She is depicted riding a lion, holding weapons in her many arms, and is revered as the destroyer of evil forces. Durga is the manifestation of Yogamaya that embodies strength, courage, and the power to eliminate darkness and ignorance.
2. **Radha**: Radha is considered the embodiment of pure devotion and love for Krishna. In the spiritual tradition of Bhakti Yoga, Radha represents the Yogamaya that unites the soul with God through the power of love and devotion. She exemplifies the highest form of divine union, where the individual soul loses itself in the bliss of communion with the Supreme.
3. **Parvati**: As the consort of Lord Shiva, Parvati is another form of Yogamaya. She represents the feminine energy that complements the destructive and transformative power of Shiva. Through her union with Shiva, Parvati facilitates the process of cosmic dissolution and rebirth, maintaining the cycle of creation.
4. **Lakshmi**: The goddess of wealth and prosperity, Lakshmi is another manifestation of Yogamaya. She represents the aspect of illusion that entices beings into the material world, offering them wealth, success, and comfort. However, for those who understand her true nature, Lakshmi becomes the force that leads to spiritual prosperity, guiding them towards divine abundance and inner fulfillment.
5. **Sita**: In the *Ramayana*, Sita, the wife of Lord Rama, is another form of Yogamaya. Her role in the epic symbolizes purity, sacrifice, and unwavering devotion. Though she faces many trials, including her abduction by Ravana, Sita remains steadfast in her dharma (righteous duty), representing the power of Yogamaya to overcome all obstacles and maintain virtue.

The Mystical Power of Yogamaya

At the heart of Yogamaya's mystique is her ability to blur the lines between illusion and reality. In the *Srimad Bhagavatam*, it is said that the entire material world, with all its forms and phenomena, is nothing but a projection of Yogamaya. It is through her power that the one infinite reality, Brahman, appears as the manifold universe, giving rise to duality—light and dark, joy and sorrow, birth and death. Yet, this duality is not the ultimate truth; it is merely a temporary stage in the soul's journey towards self-realization.

Yogamaya's influence extends not only to individuals but to the entire cosmos. She governs the workings of time (*kala*), space (*desha*), and action (*karma*), ensuring that the laws of nature and morality are upheld. Through her, the wheel of time turns, and the cycles of creation and destruction continue endlessly. At the same time, she offers a way out of this cycle for those who seek liberation. For the spiritual seeker, Yogamaya becomes the key to unlocking the ultimate reality—*Brahman*—and transcending the illusions of the material world.

Yogamaya in Modern Understanding

In today's world, where science, technology, and materialism dominate, the concept of Yogamaya remains as relevant as ever. In many ways, modern life is a reflection of Yogamaya's power. People are constantly immersed in a web of illusions—chasing after wealth, status, and pleasure, believing these things will bring lasting happiness. Yet, as ancient wisdom teaches, these are temporary illusions that distract us from the true purpose of life.

Yogamaya, therefore, can be seen as the force that governs not just the ancient myths but also the modern human experience. She is the unseen hand that guides both our struggles and our triumphs, our desires and our disillusionments. Through the lens of Yogamaya, life itself becomes a spiritual journey, where the challenges we face are not mere obstacles but opportunities for growth and awakening.

Conclusion: The Infinite Dance of Yogamaya

To truly grasp Yogamaya is to understand that life is an intricate dance between illusion and reality, where the individual soul is both the spectator and the performer. Yogamaya is the divine energy that orchestrates this dance, offering us a choice—either to remain trapped in the illusions of the material world or to transcend them and realize the eternal, unchanging truth.

In the end, Yogamaya is not merely an abstract concept or a mystical force. She is the living, breathing essence of the universe, present in every atom, every thought, and every moment of existence. To know Yogamaya is to awaken to the profound interconnectedness of all things and to recognize that behind the veil of illusion lies the infinite, boundless reality of the Divine.

Introduction : Definition of Yogamaya

In the vast ocean of Vedic literature, where mythology, philosophy, and spirituality intertwine, the concept of *Yogamaya* stands out as one of the most profound and complex mysteries. To understand Yogamaya, one must venture deep into the cosmic play orchestrated by the divine, where illusion and reality coalesce, and where time, space, and consciousness merge into one grand, infinite expanse.

To begin, let us break down the word itself. *Yoga* signifies union, connection, or a transcendental state of harmony between the individual soul (*jiva*) and the Supreme Being (*Paramatma*). *Maya*, on the other hand, refers to illusion, the magical force that veils the true nature of reality. Combined, *Yogamaya* refers to the divine power that controls both the real and the illusory aspects of existence. It is not just a form of illusion; rather, it is the supreme power that facilitates divine acts, orchestrating the entire cosmos with precision, and leading beings either towards bondage or liberation depending on their spiritual evolution.

The Origins of Yogamaya: A Mythical Perspective

To truly appreciate Yogamaya, one must travel back to the early days of the cosmos, to the realms beyond ordinary comprehension, where the eternal dance of creation, preservation, and dissolution unfolds under the gaze of the Supreme Being—Lord Vishnu. Yogamaya is often regarded as the personal energy of Vishnu or Krishna, manifesting in various forms to serve the divine will.

One of the earliest and most vivid depictions of Yogamaya appears in the story of Lord Krishna's birth. In the ancient Indian text, the *Bhagavata Purana*, we learn of a tyrannical king named Kamsa, who, upon hearing a prophecy that his sister Devaki's eighth son would be the cause of his death, imprisons her and her husband, Vasudeva. To prevent his death, Kamsa resolves to kill each of Devaki's children at birth.

But when Devaki conceives her eighth child—none other than the Supreme Lord Krishna—the divine plan comes into play. It is here that Yogamaya is invoked. As Devaki prepares to give birth, Lord Vishnu instructs her husband, Vasudeva, to exchange the newborn Krishna with a baby girl born to Yashoda and Nanda in the neighboring village of Gokul.

This baby girl is none other than Yogamaya herself, born to Yashoda in the guise of a mortal child. When Kamsa learns of the birth, he attempts to kill the child, unaware that this girl is no ordinary infant. Yogamaya, demonstrating her divine nature, slips from Kamsa's grip, ascends to the heavens, and reveals her true form as the Goddess, declaring that the one who is destined to end Kamsa's reign is already alive. Thus, Yogamaya plays her role in the divine leela (play), acting as both protector and the wielder of illusion. She deceives Kamsa while ensuring that Krishna is safe and can fulfill his destiny.

The Dual Nature of Yogamaya: Illusion and Liberation

What makes Yogamaya unique is her dual nature. On the one hand, she is the force of illusion (*maya*) that binds the individual soul to the material world, leading people to believe in the permanence of their transient lives. On the other hand, she is the guiding force (*yoga*) that can liberate the soul from this illusion, allowing one to experience union with the divine.

In the *Bhagavad Gita*, Lord Krishna tells Arjuna, "My divine energy, Yogamaya, is very difficult to overcome. But those who surrender to Me can easily cross beyond it" (Gita 7.14). Here, Krishna highlights the twofold nature of Yogamaya. For those who are immersed in ignorance, attached to their material desires and bound by their ego, Yogamaya acts as a veil, obscuring their understanding of the true nature of existence. They see the world as separate from the divine and remain entangled in the endless cycle of birth, death, and rebirth (*samsara*).

However, for the spiritually inclined, those who seek liberation (*moksha*) and the ultimate truth, Yogamaya acts as a divine bridge, leading them towards enlightenment. Through devotion, knowledge, and spiritual discipline, the veil of illusion is gradually lifted, revealing the underlying unity of all things.

Yogamaya as the Cosmic Playwright

One of the most intriguing aspects of Yogamaya is her role as the director of the cosmic drama, or *leela*. In this context, she is the power behind the play of the universe, weaving together the threads of fate, karma, and destiny. She choreographs the actions of gods, demons, and humans alike, ensuring that the cosmic balance is maintained.

In many ways, Yogamaya is akin to a master puppeteer. She manipulates the strings of illusion, allowing beings to believe that they are in control of their lives, while in reality, they are merely actors in a grander narrative. But unlike a conventional puppeteer, Yogamaya also gives her creations the power of free will, allowing them to choose their paths and face the consequences of their actions. It is through this interplay of free will and divine orchestration that the universe functions, with Yogamaya ensuring that all beings, whether bound by illusion or striving for liberation, are playing their roles in the cosmic drama.

Yogamaya and Her Manifestations

Yogamaya is not a singular entity but manifests in numerous forms, each tailored to the needs of the divine play. Some of the most well-known manifestations of Yogamaya include:

1. **Durga**: Often identified with Yogamaya, Durga is the fierce, protective mother goddess who slays demons and restores cosmic balance. She is depicted riding a lion, holding weapons in her many arms, and is revered as the destroyer of evil forces. Durga is the manifestation of Yogamaya that embodies strength, courage, and the power to eliminate darkness and ignorance.

2. **Radha**: Radha is considered the embodiment of pure devotion and love for Krishna. In the spiritual tradition of Bhakti Yoga, Radha represents the Yogamaya that unites the soul with God through the power of love and devotion. She exemplifies the highest form of divine union, where the individual soul loses itself in the bliss of communion with the Supreme.

3. **Parvati**: As the consort of Lord Shiva, Parvati is another form of Yogamaya. She represents the feminine energy that complements the destructive and transformative power of Shiva. Through her union with Shiva, Parvati facilitates the process of cosmic dissolution and rebirth, maintaining the cycle of creation.

4. **Lakshmi**: The goddess of wealth and prosperity, Lakshmi is another manifestation of Yogamaya. She represents the aspect of illusion that entices beings into the material world, offering them wealth, success, and comfort. However, for those who understand her true nature, Lakshmi becomes the force that leads to spiritual prosperity, guiding them towards divine abundance and inner fulfillment.

5. **Sita**: In the *Ramayana*, Sita, the wife of Lord Rama, is another form of Yogamaya. Her role in the epic symbolizes purity, sacrifice, and unwavering devotion. Though she faces many trials, including her abduction by Ravana, Sita remains steadfast in her dharma (righteous duty), representing the power of Yogamaya to overcome all obstacles and maintain virtue.

The Mystical Power of Yogamaya

At the heart of Yogamaya's mystique is her ability to blur the lines between illusion and reality. In the *Srimad Bhagavatam*, it is said that the entire material world, with all its forms and phenomena, is nothing but a projection of Yogamaya. It is through her power that the one infinite reality, Brahman, appears as the manifold universe, giving rise to duality—light and dark, joy and sorrow, birth and death. Yet, this duality is not the ultimate truth; it is merely a temporary stage in the soul's journey towards self-realization.

Yogamaya's influence extends not only to individuals but to the entire cosmos. She governs the workings of time (*kala*), space (*desha*), and action (*karma*), ensuring that the laws of nature and morality are upheld. Through her, the wheel of time turns, and the cycles of creation and destruction continue endlessly. At the same time, she offers a way out of this cycle for those who seek liberation. For the spiritual seeker, Yogamaya becomes the key to unlocking the ultimate reality—*Brahman*—and transcending the illusions of the material world.

Yogamaya in Modern Understanding

In today's world, where science, technology, and materialism dominate, the concept of Yogamaya remains as relevant as ever. In many ways, modern life is a reflection of Yogamaya's power. People are constantly immersed in a web of illusions—chasing after wealth, status, and pleasure, believing these things will bring lasting happiness. Yet, as ancient wisdom teaches, these are temporary illusions that distract us from the true purpose of life.

Yogamaya, therefore, can be seen as the force that governs not just the ancient myths but also the modern human experience. She is the unseen hand that guides both our struggles and our triumphs, our desires and our disillusionments. Through the lens of Yogamaya, life itself becomes a spiritual journey, where the challenges we face are not mere obstacles but opportunities for growth and awakening.

Conclusion: The Infinite Dance of Yogamaya

To truly grasp Yogamaya is to understand that life is an intricate dance between illusion and reality, where the individual soul is both the spectator and the performer. Yogamaya is the divine energy that orchestrates this dance, offering us a choice—either to remain trapped in the illusions of the material world or to transcend them and realize the eternal, unchanging truth.

In the end, Yogamaya is not merely an abstract concept or a mystical force. She is the living, breathing essence of the universe, present in every atom, every thought, and every moment of existence. To know Yogamaya is to awaken to the profound interconnectedness of all things and to recognize that behind the veil of illusion lies the infinite, boundless reality of the Divine.

- Purpose and significance of the book

In the grand narrative of human existence, the search for meaning has been a universal pursuit. Across civilizations, cultures, and epochs, we have sought answers to the fundamental questions of life: Who are we? Why are we here? What is the purpose of our existence? This book is not merely a collection of words, philosophies, or stories, but rather an invitation—a sacred calling to embark on a journey that transcends the ordinary boundaries of the mind, body, and soul. It is an exploration of the inner realms of existence, and the purpose of this book is to guide you, the reader, into the depths of spiritual understanding, self-realization, and the discovery of your own divinity.

The significance of this book lies not in its mere intellectual appeal or scholarly wisdom, but in its potential to transform your perspective of life. It aims to illuminate the profound truth that beneath the surface of the material world lies a deeper reality—a reality that can be accessed not through the senses but through the awakening of consciousness. It is a map, a guide, a key to unlocking the mysteries of existence that have perplexed humanity for millennia.

A Story of Awakening

Imagine, for a moment, that you are living in a small village surrounded by dense forests. The people in your village believe that the forest is all there is—that beyond the trees, there is nothing but endless darkness. They spend their days cultivating the land, raising families, and trading goods, yet a deep sense of dissatisfaction pervades their lives. Though they seem happy, deep within, there is an unspoken yearning for something more, something beyond the tangible.

One day, you hear of a wise sage who lives at the edge of the forest. Intrigued by tales of his wisdom and the secrets he holds, you set out to find him. As you approach his humble dwelling, you are filled with both excitement and trepidation. You have so many questions: Is there really something beyond the forest? What lies in the unknown expanse beyond? Why do you feel this inexplicable longing for something greater?

The sage welcomes you with a serene smile and offers you a seat by the fire. As the flames flicker and dance, casting shadows on the walls of the cave, he begins to speak. His voice is calm, yet powerful. He speaks not of the forest, the village, or the daily struggles of life, but of a reality far beyond your comprehension. He tells you that the world you see is but a small fragment of a much larger, infinite existence. He speaks of realms of consciousness, of illusions that bind the mind, and of a deeper, eternal truth that lies within you.

As you listen, something inside you stirs. You begin to realize that the life you've known—the life you believed to be complete—is but a shadow of a much grander reality. The sage's words resonate with an ancient memory, something you've always known but had forgotten. The journey has just begun, and this book is the path.

The Purpose: A Spiritual Awakening

The primary purpose of this book is to guide you towards that same awakening. Just as the sage in the story led you to question the boundaries of your known world, this book aims to encourage you to question the limitations of your understanding. It invites you to step beyond the material, beyond the apparent, and delve into the depths of spiritual knowledge that has been passed down through the ages.

This book is written for those who are ready to explore the deeper questions of existence, those who feel a sense of discontent with the superficial answers provided by the material world. It is for those who have felt the tug of something greater—an inexplicable yearning to understand the mysteries of life and the cosmos.

But what does it mean to awaken? In the context of this book, awakening refers to the process of becoming conscious of the deeper truths that govern reality. It means realizing that the world we perceive through our senses is only a small part of the vast tapestry of existence. It means understanding that we are not mere physical bodies bound by time and space, but spiritual beings connected to the infinite source of all creation.

Awakening is not just a philosophical idea; it is a lived experience. It is the realization that the soul—the true essence of who we are—exists beyond the confines of the ego, beyond the attachments and desires that define our worldly lives. To awaken is to see through the illusion of separateness and recognize the interconnectedness of all life. It is to embrace the truth that the divine resides not in some distant heaven, but within the very core of our being.

The Role of Yogamaya in Our Journey

As we explore the purpose of this book, we must also understand the significance of the central concept it presents—*Yogamaya*. In the grand drama of life, Yogamaya plays a pivotal role. She is the force that both conceals and reveals the truth. On one hand, she is the illusion that binds us to the material world, causing us to believe in the permanence of our transient lives. On the other hand, she is the divine power that leads us towards liberation, guiding us to transcend the illusions of the ego and discover the eternal reality.

Through Yogamaya, we experience the duality of existence—joy and sorrow, birth and death, light and darkness. But the ultimate purpose of Yogamaya is not to trap us in this duality; it is to help us transcend it. She is the cosmic force that orchestrates the interplay of illusion and reality, allowing us to navigate the complexities of life while offering us a path to liberation.

This book serves as a guide to understanding Yogamaya's role in our lives. It explains how we are caught in the web of illusion and how we can break free from it. It shows us that while the material world may appear real and all-consuming, it is, in fact, a fleeting dream. Beyond this dream lies the eternal truth, the ultimate reality, which can only be experienced through the awakening of consciousness.

The Significance: A Call to Transformation

The significance of this book lies in its potential to transform your life. It is not a book that seeks to impart mere knowledge or intellectual understanding; rather, it seeks to inspire a profound inner transformation. The wisdom contained within these pages is not theoretical; it is practical, applicable to the everyday experiences of life.

In the story of the sage and the village, the moment of transformation came when the seeker began to see beyond the forest, beyond the limitations of his mind. Similarly, this book aims to ignite that moment of transformation within you. It encourages you to look beyond the surface of your life, beyond the distractions and desires that occupy your mind, and to seek the deeper truths that lie within.

Transformation begins with awareness. As you read through the pages of this book, you will be encouraged to reflect on your own life. What illusions have you been holding onto? What attachments have been keeping you bound to the material world? What fears, desires, and ego-driven pursuits have been clouding your vision of the truth? This book will gently guide you to confront these questions, not with judgment, but with compassion and understanding.

Through the stories, teachings, and insights presented in this book, you will be led on a journey of self-discovery. You will learn that the path to liberation is not an external quest but an internal one. The answers you seek do not lie in the world outside but within your own consciousness. As you peel back the layers of illusion, you will begin to glimpse the radiant light of your true self, the divine essence that has been waiting to be uncovered.

The Book as a Spiritual Companion

This book is not meant to be read once and then set aside. It is intended to be a lifelong companion on your spiritual journey. The teachings within these pages are timeless, rooted in the ancient wisdom of the Vedas, the Upanishads, and other sacred texts. Yet, they are also deeply relevant to the modern world, offering guidance for navigating the complexities of contemporary life while staying rooted in spiritual truth.

The significance of this book also lies in its accessibility. It is written in a way that speaks to readers of all backgrounds and levels of spiritual experience. Whether you are just beginning your spiritual journey or have been on the path for many years, this book offers insights that can help deepen your understanding and expand your consciousness.

The teachings of Yogamaya, the process of awakening, and the journey to self-realization are universal truths that transcend cultural, religious, and philosophical boundaries. They speak to the very essence of what it means to be human, to live, to suffer, to seek, and ultimately, to transcend.

A Conclusion: The Infinite Quest

In conclusion, the purpose and significance of this book are intertwined in its mission to guide you towards a deeper understanding of life's ultimate truth. It is a book about liberation—liberation from the illusions that bind us to the material world, from the fears and desires that cloud our vision, and from the ignorance that keeps us from realizing our own divinity.

But this book is not an endpoint; it is a beginning. It is an invitation to embark on the infinite quest for self-realization, a journey that continues beyond the pages of this text and into the very fabric of your existence. As you read, reflect, and meditate on the teachings within, you will begin to see that the ultimate purpose of life is not found in the external world, but within your own soul.

May this book serve as a beacon of light on your path, guiding you towards the realization of your true nature and the infinite reality that lies beyond the veil of illusion.

- Overview of themes and concepts to be covered

The journey you are about to embark upon through the pages of this book is unlike any other. It is a voyage into the depths of the human soul, a pilgrimage that spans the inner landscapes of consciousness, reality, and the cosmos itself. As you proceed through each chapter, you will encounter themes and concepts that, though ancient in their origins, are timeless in their relevance. These are not merely abstract ideas to ponder but essential truths that have the power to reshape the very fabric of your understanding of life, existence, and the divine.

At its core, this book explores the intricate dance between illusion and reality, between the material and the spiritual, and between ignorance and enlightenment. Through a careful examination of the interplay between these dualities, we will unravel the mysteries that have captivated the minds of sages, mystics, and seekers throughout history. In this overview, we will explore the key themes and concepts that will serve as the guiding stars on this profound spiritual journey.

Each theme is interconnected, forming a rich tapestry that weaves together philosophy, mythology, and practical spiritual wisdom. Let us begin by diving deep into these central concepts.

1. The Nature of Reality: Illusion and Truth

The first and perhaps the most fundamental theme explored in this book is the nature of reality itself. This is the bedrock upon which all other spiritual insights rest, for without understanding what reality is—and more importantly, what it is not—we cannot hope to grasp the deeper truths of existence.

In the spiritual traditions of the East, particularly in the Vedic and Upanishadic teachings, reality is understood to exist on multiple levels. There is the material world that we perceive through our senses, which is transient and ever-changing, and then there is the deeper, eternal reality that is unchanging and absolute. The material world, governed by *Maya*—the illusion—appears to be real, but it is, in fact, a temporary projection, much like a dream.

Throughout the book, we will explore the concept of *Maya*, the veil that shrouds our understanding of true reality. We will examine how this illusion binds us to the cycle of birth, death, and rebirth (*samsara*), creating the false perception that we are separate from the divine. But within this illusion also lies the opportunity for liberation, for behind the veil of Maya is the eternal truth of *Brahman*—the ultimate reality, the source of all existence, which is beyond time, space, and causality.

We will delve into ancient texts such as the *Upanishads* and the *Bhagavad Gita*, which reveal that the world we perceive through our senses is not the true reality but merely a reflection of the infinite consciousness. Understanding this is the first step toward spiritual awakening, and this book will guide you through that process, helping you see through the illusion to glimpse the ultimate truth.

2. Yogamaya: The Power of Divine Illusion

One of the most important and unique themes in this book is the exploration of *Yogamaya*. As we discussed in earlier chapters, Yogamaya is not merely a concept of illusion, but the divine force that both veils and reveals the truth. Yogamaya is the feminine energy, the creative and protective power of the divine that orchestrates the dance of the cosmos. She is the force behind the *leela* (divine play) of the universe, guiding the souls of beings towards either bondage or liberation.

Yogamaya plays a dual role in the spiritual journey. On the one hand, she creates the world of duality, where the soul experiences joy and sorrow, gain and loss, birth and death. This world is the field in which we live out our karma, where we make choices that either bind us further into illusion or free us from it. On the other hand, Yogamaya also serves as the guiding light for those who seek to transcend the illusion. For the devotee who surrenders to the divine, Yogamaya becomes the path of enlightenment, dissolving the barriers of illusion and leading the soul toward the ultimate truth.

This theme of Yogamaya will be explored through the myths and stories of the Hindu tradition, particularly in the life of Lord Krishna, who is often seen as the embodiment of Yogamaya's power. Through these stories, we will see how Yogamaya manifests both as the protector and the revealer of truth, how she orchestrates the divine play, and how her energy can be harnessed for spiritual awakening.

3. The Soul's Journey: Karma and Samsara

No exploration of spiritual philosophy is complete without a deep understanding of *karma* and *samsara*. These concepts form the very foundation of the soul's journey through countless lifetimes, shaping the experiences we undergo in the material world. Karma, the law of cause and effect, governs the actions of all beings. Every thought, word, and deed produces an effect, whether immediate or in a future lifetime, and this ripple of consequences determines the nature of our experiences in this life and beyond.

In this book, we will take an in-depth look at the intricacies of karma—how it binds the soul, how it accumulates across lifetimes, and how it can be transcended. Karma is not merely a system of reward and punishment; rather, it is the force that teaches us the consequences of our actions, allowing us to learn, grow, and ultimately evolve. Through understanding the mechanics of karma, we can begin to take conscious control of our actions, directing them toward spiritual growth rather than entanglement in the material world.

The concept of samsara, the cycle of birth, death, and rebirth, is intricately linked to karma. As long as our karma remains unresolved, we continue to reincarnate in various forms, experiencing the joys and sorrows of existence. The goal of the spiritual journey is to break free from this cycle by achieving *moksha*—liberation from samsara and union with the divine. The exploration of samsara and karma in this book will provide practical tools for understanding how we can escape the endless loop of reincarnation and move toward spiritual freedom.

4. Liberation: The Path to Moksha

At the heart of every spiritual tradition lies the quest for *moksha*, or liberation. In the Hindu and Buddhist traditions, moksha represents the final goal of human existence—the release from the cycle of samsara and the realization of the soul's true nature as one with Brahman, the ultimate reality.

In this book, the concept of moksha is presented not as an abstract or distant ideal, but as an achievable state of being. We will explore various paths to liberation, from the path of knowledge (*jnana yoga*) to the path of devotion (*bhakti yoga*) and the path of selfless action (*karma yoga*). Each of these paths offers a unique approach to breaking free from the chains of illusion and realizing the divine within.

Through stories, teachings, and practical advice, we will uncover the essence of moksha—not merely as a future state but as a present reality that can be experienced in this lifetime. We will learn that liberation is not the annihilation of the self but the transcendence of the ego, the realization that the individual soul is, and always has been, one with the infinite consciousness.

5. Bhakti: The Power of Devotion and Divine Love

One of the most profound themes explored in this book is the power of *bhakti*—devotion and love for the divine. Bhakti is often considered the most accessible path to spiritual realization, as it does not require intellectual knowledge or physical austerities but a pure, open heart filled with love for God. Through the stories of saints, sages, and mystics who have walked the path of devotion, we will explore how bhakti leads to union with the divine, dissolving the barriers of the ego and awakening the soul to its eternal nature.

Bhakti is the path of surrender, where the seeker offers all their thoughts, actions, and emotions to the divine. It is the realization that love is the most powerful force in the universe and that through love, the soul can transcend the illusions of the material world. Bhakti teaches us that God is not a distant or impersonal force, but a loving presence that resides within each of us. This theme will resonate deeply with readers who seek to connect with the divine through love and devotion rather than intellectual understanding.

6. The Role of the Guru: The Spiritual Guide

In the spiritual journey, the role of the *guru*, or spiritual teacher, is of paramount importance. The guru is the guide who has already traversed the path to enlightenment and can lead the seeker through the complexities of the spiritual journey. In this book, we will explore the significance of the guru in spiritual traditions, particularly in the context of Yogamaya.

The guru is not just a human teacher but a channel through which divine wisdom flows. The true guru embodies the energy of Yogamaya, helping the seeker navigate the illusions of the material world and leading them toward self-realization. This theme will delve into the sacred relationship between guru and disciple, offering insights into how one can recognize and receive guidance from a genuine spiritual teacher.

7. Meditation and Mindfulness: Practices for Awakening

Spiritual philosophy alone is not enough to lead to awakening; it must be accompanied by practice. This book places a strong emphasis on the importance of meditation and mindfulness as essential tools for spiritual growth. These practices allow the seeker to quiet the mind, transcend the distractions of the material world, and connect with the deeper layers of consciousness.

Through various forms of meditation—whether focusing on breath, mantra, or divine images—this book will provide practical guidance for cultivating inner stillness and awareness. Mindfulness, or the practice of living in the present moment, is another key theme that will be explored. By practicing mindfulness, we learn to observe the world without attachment, seeing through the illusion of separateness and recognizing the divine presence in all things.

8. Interconnectedness and Unity: The Oneness of All Existence

One of the most transformative themes explored in this book is the concept of *oneness*—the realization that all beings, all forms, and all of existence are interconnected and part of the same divine reality. This understanding dissolves the illusion of separateness that binds us to the ego and opens the door to a deeper experience of love, compassion, and unity with all of creation.

The theme of interconnectedness will be woven throughout the book, reminding us that the material world is not something to be rejected but embraced as a manifestation of the divine. By seeing the world through the eyes of unity, we can transcend the dualities of existence and live from a place of unconditional love and acceptance.

9. Practical Spirituality: Integrating Wisdom into Daily Life

Finally, this book will address the question of how to integrate spiritual wisdom into daily life. The journey toward self-realization is not separate from the everyday experiences of work, relationships, and challenges. This book will offer practical advice on how to live a life grounded in spiritual awareness, even in the midst of the material world.

Themes such as detachment, non-judgment, compassion, and selfless service will be explored as tools for bringing the insights of spiritual practice into every aspect of life. This book is not just about philosophy; it is about transformation—how to live a life that is aligned with the highest truth, regardless of external circumstances.

A Conclusion: The Infinite Path

The themes and concepts explored in this book are not static ideas but living principles that will unfold as you progress through the spiritual journey. Each theme will be revisited, deepened, and expanded as you move through the chapters, providing a comprehensive understanding of the path to self-realization.

This book is a roadmap, a guide to the infinite path that lies ahead of you. As you delve into these themes, you will discover that the journey is never truly over—each insight, each experience, and each realization opens the door to even deeper layers of truth.

May these themes serve as beacons of light, guiding you toward the eternal truth that lies beyond the illusions of the material world. Let this book be your companion on the path to liberation, offering wisdom, inspiration, and practical guidance as you embark on the most important journey of all—the journey toward the realization of your own divine nature.

Chapter 1: Understanding Yogamaya

• Historical and philosophical context

In the beginning, before time and space took shape, before the stars flickered into existence or the earth began its slow dance around the sun, there existed only one—an infinite, formless, and boundless consciousness. This was *Brahman*, the ultimate reality, the essence of everything that was, is, and ever will be. Brahman, in its purest state, was unmanifest, beyond the comprehension of human mind and senses. It was the silent, eternal witness to all that would eventually unfold in the universe. But in its vast stillness, Brahman harbored the potential for creation. This is where the story of *Yogamaya* begins.

Yogamaya, the divine force of illusion and truth, emerges from Brahman as its creative power, its cosmic energy. To truly understand Yogamaya, we must first delve into the ancient history and philosophy that gave rise to this profound concept. Her origins lie in the vast expanse of spiritual teachings that evolved thousands of years ago in the Indian subcontinent, in the sacred texts and philosophies of the Vedas, the Upanishads, and the Bhagavad Gita. Over the millennia, Yogamaya has been revered, studied, and worshipped as a manifestation of the divine feminine energy, the force that creates, sustains, and eventually dissolves the universe.

The Vedic Age: The Birth of Cosmic Knowledge

Our journey begins in the early Vedic period, approximately 1500 to 500 BCE. This era is marked by the composition of the Vedas, the oldest sacred scriptures of Hinduism, which form the foundation of Indian spiritual thought. The Vedas are not just religious texts but are a record of the cosmic knowledge that the ancient sages, or *rishis*, perceived during deep states of meditation. The rishis saw the universe as a vast, interconnected web of energy, with every element and being part of an intricate cosmic order known as *Rta*.

Though the concept of Yogamaya as we understand it today was not fully formed in the Vedic age, the seeds of this idea were already present. The Vedas speak of the divine energy that pervades all of creation, an energy that is both the source of life and the force that binds beings to the material world. In the Rig Veda, one of the earliest texts, there are hymns that describe the universe as a play of illusion and reality, where the divine is both hidden and revealed.

In the Vedic worldview, the material world is not seen as false or illusory in a negative sense, but rather as part of the divine play of *leela*, the cosmic game. This playful creation is made possible by the veiling power of the divine, which conceals the ultimate reality from ordinary perception, allowing beings to experience life as separate individuals. This veiling power is the essence of what would later be recognized as Yogamaya.

The Upanishads: The Philosophical Foundations of Yogamaya

As we move forward in history, the teachings of the Upanishads, composed between 800 and 200 BCE, take us deeper into the philosophical underpinnings of Yogamaya. The Upanishads are considered the philosophical heart of the Vedas, offering profound insights into the nature of reality, the self (*Atman*), and the ultimate truth (*Brahman*). It is in these texts that the tension between illusion and reality is explored with greater depth and subtlety.

In the Upanishads, the material world is described as *Maya*, an illusion that conceals the true nature of Brahman. Maya is not a denial of the existence of the world, but rather a recognition that what we perceive is not the ultimate reality. It is through the veil of Maya that we experience the dualities of life—birth and death, joy and sorrow, success and failure. Yet behind this veil lies the eternal truth of oneness, where all distinctions dissolve, and only pure consciousness remains.

The famous teaching from the *Chandogya Upanishad* declares, "*Tat Tvam Asi*" ("Thou art that"), a reminder that the individual self is not separate from the ultimate reality but is one with it. However, due to the power of Maya, we perceive ourselves as distinct and separate beings, caught in the web of time, space, and causality. It is here that Yogamaya comes into focus. Yogamaya is the dynamic, creative aspect of Maya, the force that not only veils the truth but also holds the potential to reveal it.

The Upanishads also introduce the concept of *avidya*, or ignorance, which is the root cause of our entanglement in the illusions of the world. Avidya prevents us from recognizing our true nature as divine, keeping us bound to the material plane. But the same force that binds us—Yogamaya—also holds the key to liberation. Through spiritual knowledge (*jnana*), devotion (*bhakti*), and selfless action (*karma*), one can pierce the veil of Yogamaya and realize the oneness of all existence.

Yogamaya in the Bhagavad Gita: The Divine Play of Krishna

As we continue to trace the evolution of Yogamaya, we arrive at one of the most significant spiritual texts of all time: the *Bhagavad Gita*. Composed around the 2nd century BCE as part of the epic *Mahabharata*, the Bhagavad Gita presents a dialogue between Prince Arjuna and the god Krishna on the eve of a great battle. This text offers profound teachings on duty, righteousness, and the nature of reality, and it is here that Yogamaya assumes a more defined role.

Krishna, the incarnation of the supreme deity Vishnu, embodies the divine energy of Yogamaya. In the Bhagavad Gita, Krishna reveals that the entire universe is his creation, sustained by his power, and ultimately dissolved back into him. He explains that the material world is governed by his *prakriti* (nature), which is a manifestation of Yogamaya. Through Yogamaya, Krishna creates the world of duality and multiplicity, allowing souls to experience life, death, and rebirth. But he also reminds Arjuna that this world is not the final reality; it is a temporary play, a cosmic drama designed to teach souls the lessons they need to evolve spiritually.

Krishna's teachings on Yogamaya are particularly profound when he explains that while he appears to be part of the world, taking on a human form and interacting with beings, he is, in fact, beyond it. He says in Chapter 9, Verse 4 of the Gita: "By me, in my unmanifested form, this entire universe is pervaded. All beings are in me, but I am not in them." Here, Krishna speaks of his transcendence, reminding us that while Yogamaya creates the illusion of separation and multiplicity, the ultimate truth is that all beings are one with the divine.

One of the most significant moments in the Bhagavad Gita is when Krishna reveals his *Vishvarupa*—his universal form—to Arjuna. In this moment, the veil of Yogamaya is temporarily lifted, and Arjuna is able to see Krishna not as a human form but as the infinite, all-encompassing reality. This vision is both awe-inspiring and terrifying, as it reveals the vastness and power of the divine, showing that all creation, destruction, and rebirth are part of the same cosmic cycle orchestrated by Yogamaya.

Philosophical Interpretations: Advaita Vedanta and Yogamaya

As we move into the classical period of Indian philosophy, the concept of Yogamaya continues to be explored and refined by various schools of thought. One of the most influential interpretations comes from the *Advaita Vedanta* school, founded by the philosopher Adi Shankaracharya in the 8th century CE. Advaita Vedanta is a non-dualistic philosophy that teaches that the ultimate reality is Brahman, and that the individual self (*Atman*) is not separate from Brahman but identical to it.

In Advaita Vedanta, Yogamaya is understood as the force that creates the illusion of duality—the appearance that there is a distinction between the self and the divine. According to Shankaracharya, this illusion is the result of ignorance (*avidya*), which causes us to identify with the body, mind, and ego rather than with the infinite consciousness that is our true nature. The purpose of spiritual practice, in this view, is to transcend the illusions of Yogamaya and realize the oneness of all existence.

Shankaracharya's teachings emphasize that while the world of Yogamaya appears real to those who are caught in ignorance, it is ultimately an illusion. However, this does not mean that the world is meaningless or to be rejected. Rather, it is to be understood as a temporary play, a *leela*, through which the soul learns and evolves. By recognizing the illusory nature of the world and turning inward to seek the eternal truth of Brahman, one can achieve *moksha*, or liberation from the cycle of birth and rebirth.

The Role of Yogamaya in Devotional Traditions

While Advaita Vedanta focuses on the philosophical aspects of Yogamaya, the devotional traditions of Hinduism offer a more personal and intimate understanding of this divine power. In the *Bhakti* (devotional) movements that flourished in India from the 6th century CE onward, Yogamaya is seen not just as an abstract force but as the compassionate, loving energy of the divine, manifesting in various forms to guide and protect devotees.

In the devotional worship of Krishna, for example, Yogamaya is revered as the power that allows the devotee to experience the divine presence in the world. Through the practice of bhakti, the devotee surrenders to the will of Yogamaya, trusting that her illusions are part of the divine play that leads the soul toward union with God. In this sense, Yogamaya is not merely a force of illusion but also a path to enlightenment. She creates the conditions in which the soul can awaken to its true nature, offering both the challenge of illusion and the grace of liberation.

Conclusion: Yogamaya as the Key to Understanding Reality

As we conclude this chapter, it becomes clear that Yogamaya is not simply a concept confined to ancient texts and philosophies; it is a living, dynamic force that continues to shape our understanding of reality. Yogamaya is the divine veil that both conceals and reveals the truth. She is the power that creates the illusion of separation while also providing the means to transcend that illusion.

In the chapters that follow, we will explore how Yogamaya operates in the lives of individuals, how she manifests in the stories of gods and goddesses, and how her energy can be harnessed for spiritual awakening. As you journey deeper into the mysteries of Yogamaya, you will come to see that she is not only the key to understanding the nature of reality but also the guide who leads us back to the source of all existence—the infinite, formless, and eternal Brahman.

- **Roots in Hindu scriptures**

The ancient lands of the Indian subcontinent have long been regarded as the cradle of spiritual wisdom, a place where the mysteries of the universe have been contemplated and explored for millennia. It is within this rich tapestry of history and culture that the concept of *Yogamaya* emerges—a concept woven intricately into the very fabric of Hindu philosophy, spirituality, and the scriptures that have guided countless seekers on the path to enlightenment. To fully understand the depth and significance of Yogamaya, we must travel back in time, tracing her roots through the oldest and most revered texts in Hinduism—the *Vedas*, the *Upanishads*, the *Puranas*, and the *Bhagavad Gita*.

The Vedic Origins: The First Glimpse of the Divine Power

Our journey begins with the *Vedas*, a collection of hymns and sacred verses composed thousands of years ago by the ancient seers known as *rishis*. These texts, which are the oldest scriptures in the Hindu tradition, were not merely written works but revelations received by the rishis in deep states of meditation. The Vedas are divided into four main collections—the *Rig Veda*, *Yajur Veda*, *Sama Veda*, and *Atharva Veda*. While Yogamaya as a fully developed concept does not explicitly appear in these texts, the seeds of her existence are planted here.

The Vedic worldview is one of profound interconnectedness, where the material world and the spiritual world are seen as reflections of a higher cosmic order known as *Rta*. This order is sustained by the gods and goddesses who represent various forces of nature—Agni, the god of fire; Indra, the god of storms; Varuna, the god of the waters; and many others. But behind these deities lies a deeper truth, an unmanifest force that governs the universe. This force is *Prakriti*, the primordial energy from which all creation arises. It is Prakriti that would later evolve into the concept of Maya and, more specifically, Yogamaya.

In the hymns of the Rig Veda, there are allusions to this hidden power, often described as the force that governs creation and destruction, light and darkness. One hymn in particular, the *Nasadiya Sukta* (the Hymn of Creation), contemplates the mystery of existence itself, questioning how the universe came into being and what force lies behind it:

"Then was not non-existent nor existent:
There was no realm of air, no sky beyond it.
What covered in, and where? And what gave shelter?
Was water there, unfathomed depth of water?"

The Nasadiya Sukta reflects the Vedic understanding that the origins of the universe are shrouded in mystery, with a creative power veiling the ultimate reality. This veiling power, though unnamed in the Vedas, is the earliest hint of what would later be known as *Maya*, the force that both conceals and reveals the truth. Yogamaya, as a more refined concept, would emerge later, but her essence is present here—in the recognition that the world we perceive is not the full truth, but a manifestation of a deeper, unseen reality.

The Upanishads: The Emergence of Maya and Yogamaya

As the spiritual teachings of the Vedas evolved, they gave birth to a new body of philosophical writings known as the *Upanishads*. The Upanishads, composed between 800 BCE and 200 BCE, represent the culmination of Vedic thought and form the basis of Hindu metaphysics. It is in these texts that the concept of *Maya* takes on a more defined and central role, and the deeper nature of Yogamaya begins to emerge.

The Upanishads are concerned with the nature of reality, the self (*Atman*), and the ultimate truth (*Brahman*). One of the key teachings of the Upanishads is that the material world we perceive with our senses is not the ultimate reality, but rather an illusion—a projection of Maya. Maya is described as the force that creates the appearance of multiplicity and separateness in the world, making us believe that we are distinct individuals rather than expressions of the one, infinite Brahman.

In the *Mandukya Upanishad*, the analogy of the dream is used to explain Maya's role in veiling the truth. Just as a dream appears real to the dreamer while they are asleep, the material world appears real to those who are caught in the illusion of Maya. But just as the dream dissolves upon waking, the illusion of the material world is dispelled when one attains spiritual knowledge and realizes the oneness of all existence.

Yet, Maya is not simply a force of illusion. It is also a force of creation, a dynamic energy that gives rise to the universe. This creative aspect of Maya is where Yogamaya comes into play. While Maya is often associated with ignorance (*avidya*) and the bondage of the soul, Yogamaya is the divine, conscious aspect of Maya—an energy that can be both a veil and a revelation. Yogamaya is the power through which the divine manifests in the world, creating the conditions for spiritual growth and eventual liberation.

The *Kena Upanishad* offers a glimpse into the dual nature of this power:

"That which cannot be seen with the eye, but by which the eye can see—know that to be Brahman. That which cannot be heard with the ear, but by which the ear can hear—know that to be Brahman."

Here, we see that the divine energy, while hidden, is also the very force that makes perception possible. Yogamaya operates in a similar way—she conceals the ultimate truth, but she is also the key to revealing it. Through the practice of meditation, devotion, and self-inquiry, one can transcend the illusions of Maya and come to experience the deeper reality that Yogamaya both hides and illuminates.

The Puranas: Yogamaya as the Divine Goddess

As we move forward in time, we encounter a new genre of Hindu scripture—the *Puranas*. The Puranas, composed between 300 CE and 1500 CE, are a vast collection of stories, myths, and legends that describe the creation of the universe, the genealogies of gods and goddesses, and the deeds of great heroes and saints. It is in the Puranas that the figure of Yogamaya begins to take on a more personal and mythological form, often depicted as a goddess with the power to create, sustain, and dissolve the universe.

One of the most significant references to Yogamaya in the Puranas is found in the *Bhagavata Purana*, where she is described as a manifestation of the divine feminine energy, *Shakti*. In this text, Yogamaya is portrayed as a powerful goddess who plays a central role in the life of Lord Krishna, one of the most beloved deities in Hinduism.

According to the Bhagavata Purana, when Krishna was born to the mortal woman Devaki, the tyrant king Kamsa sought to kill him, fearing a prophecy that foretold his downfall at the hands of Devaki's eighth son. To protect Krishna, the divine power of Yogamaya intervened. On the night of Krishna's birth, Yogamaya took the form of a child and was exchanged with Krishna by his father, Vasudeva. When Kamsa tried to kill this child, she transformed into the goddess Yogamaya, escaping his grasp and warning him of his impending doom.

In this story, Yogamaya acts as both protector and revealer. She conceals Krishna's divine identity, allowing him to grow up in safety, while simultaneously playing a role in the cosmic drama that would lead to Kamsa's defeat. This narrative highlights Yogamaya's dual function as the force that both hides and reveals the divine plan.

The *Devi Bhagavata Purana*, another important text, further explores Yogamaya's role as a goddess. In this text, she is described as the sister of Krishna, the embodiment of the supreme divine power that governs the universe. She is revered as a compassionate and powerful force who aids in the liberation of souls from the cycle of birth and death.

The Bhagavad Gita: Yogamaya in the Teachings of Krishna

No discussion of Yogamaya would be complete without delving into the *Bhagavad Gita*, one of the most profound and widely studied spiritual texts in the world. The Bhagavad Gita, composed around the 2nd century BCE, is a 700-verse dialogue between Prince Arjuna and the god Krishna, set on the battlefield of Kurukshetra. In this sacred conversation, Krishna reveals deep spiritual truths to Arjuna, addressing the nature of life, duty, and the self.

Yogamaya plays a pivotal role in Krishna's teachings in the Bhagavad Gita. Krishna explains to Arjuna that the material world is governed by his divine energy, which manifests as Yogamaya. He says in Chapter 7, Verse 25:

"I am not manifest to all, veiled by my Yogamaya. The ignorant do not know me as the unborn and imperishable."

Here, Krishna reveals that his true nature is hidden by Yogamaya, the divine power that creates the illusion of separateness and individuality. This illusion is necessary for the functioning of the world, but it also creates the conditions for ignorance and attachment. However, Krishna also explains that through devotion and selfless action, one can transcend the illusions of Yogamaya and come to know the divine truth.

In Chapter 11, Krishna further illustrates the power of Yogamaya when he grants Arjuna a vision of his universal form, the *Vishvarupa*. In this awe-inspiring vision, Arjuna sees Krishna as the infinite, all-encompassing reality, with countless forms, faces, and arms, encompassing the entire cosmos. This moment is a profound revelation, where the veil of Yogamaya is temporarily lifted, allowing Arjuna to see the true nature of the divine.

Krishna's teachings in the Bhagavad Gita emphasize that while Yogamaya creates the illusion of separation, it is also the force that leads the soul back to unity with the divine. Through surrender to the will of the divine, one can transcend the illusions of the material world and realize the oneness of all existence.

Conclusion: Yogamaya's Eternal Presence in the Scriptures

As we conclude this chapter, it becomes clear that Yogamaya is not a mere philosophical abstraction, but a living, dynamic force deeply embedded in the sacred texts of Hinduism. From the earliest hymns of the Vedas to the profound teachings of the Upanishads, from the mythological narratives of the Puranas to the spiritual wisdom of the Bhagavad Gita, Yogamaya is present at every stage of the journey.

She is the veil that conceals the truth and the key to its revelation. She is both the force that binds us to the material world and the power that liberates us from it. Through her, the divine plan unfolds, guiding souls on the path of spiritual evolution. In the chapters to come, we will explore how this timeless force operates in the lives of individuals, how she manifests in the myths and legends of the gods and goddesses, and how her energy can be invoked for transformation and enlightenment. The journey into the mysteries of Yogamaya has only just begun.

- **Comparison with similar concepts in other traditions**

As we venture deeper into the exploration of *Yogamaya*, it becomes essential to step beyond the boundaries of Hinduism and examine how similar concepts have emerged in other spiritual and philosophical traditions around the world. Though Yogamaya is deeply rooted in Hindu cosmology, the themes of illusion, divine power, and the relationship between the material and spiritual realms are universal. They echo across the mystical teachings of different cultures, from ancient Eastern philosophies to Western religious thought.

In this chapter, we will journey across time and space to explore how Yogamaya, the divine power of illusion and revelation, finds resonance in other traditions. By comparing Yogamaya to similar concepts in Buddhism, ancient Greek philosophy, Christian mysticism, Sufism, and even modern philosophical thought, we can gain a richer understanding of her universal relevance. Through these comparisons, we will discover that while the names, symbols, and interpretations may differ, the fundamental truths remain the same: reality is more than what meets the eye, and the path to liberation involves transcending the illusions that bind us to the material world.

Buddhism: Maya and Samsara

One of the closest parallels to Yogamaya in another spiritual tradition can be found in *Buddhism*, particularly in the concepts of *Maya* and *Samsara*. The Buddha, born in the same cultural milieu as the sages of the Upanishads, also grappled with the problem of illusion and suffering, though he approached it from a different perspective.

In Buddhism, *Maya* refers to the deceptive nature of the material world. Just as in Hinduism, Maya in Buddhism is not simply a lie or falsehood but a veil that obscures the deeper truth of existence. The Buddha taught that all conditioned phenomena—everything we perceive through our senses—is *impermanent* and *insubstantial*. We mistake these fleeting forms for reality, and as a result, we become attached to them. This attachment leads to suffering, or *dukkha*, which is the central problem in Buddhist thought.

The cycle of birth, death, and rebirth, known as *Samsara*, is intimately tied to the illusion of Maya. As long as beings remain caught in the delusions of the ego, they continue to cycle through Samsara, experiencing suffering and dissatisfaction. Liberation, or *Nirvana*, is achieved when one sees through the illusion of Maya and realizes the truth of *Sunyata*, or emptiness. Sunyata refers to the understanding that all things are empty of inherent, independent existence. This realization leads to the cessation of attachment and the end of suffering.

While Yogamaya in Hinduism is often seen as both an obstacle and a means of spiritual progress, in Buddhism, Maya is primarily seen as an obstacle. Yet, both traditions agree on the central idea: the world we perceive is not the ultimate reality, and transcending this illusion is the key to liberation.

Interestingly, the figure of Yogamaya makes an appearance in Buddhist lore as well. In certain Buddhist texts, Yogamaya is regarded as the goddess of illusion, playing a role in the birth of the Buddha. Similar to her role in the birth of Krishna, Yogamaya is said to have intervened in the Buddha's birth, helping to conceal his true divine nature until the time was right for him to reveal his teachings to the world. This commonality between Hindu and Buddhist narratives illustrates the shared cultural and spiritual heritage from which both traditions arose.

Ancient Greek Philosophy: Plato's Allegory of the Cave

Moving from the East to the West, we find that the ancient Greeks also grappled with the question of illusion and reality. Perhaps the most famous expression of this theme in Western philosophy is *Plato's Allegory of the Cave*, found in his seminal work *The Republic*.

In this allegory, Plato describes a group of prisoners who have been chained inside a cave for their entire lives. They are forced to face the wall of the cave and can see only the shadows of objects cast by a fire behind them. For these prisoners, the shadows are the only reality they know. They believe that the shadows are the true forms of things, unaware that there is an entire world outside the cave that they cannot see.

One day, a prisoner is freed and steps outside the cave into the sunlight. At first, he is blinded by the light and disoriented, but gradually he begins to see the true forms of the objects that were casting the shadows. He realizes that the reality he had known inside the cave was an illusion, a mere reflection of the truth. He returns to the cave to try to enlighten the other prisoners, but they resist, unwilling to let go of the shadows that they have come to accept as reality.

Plato's allegory mirrors the concept of Yogamaya in many ways. The cave represents the world of illusion—the material world that we perceive with our senses. The shadows on the wall are the fleeting, impermanent forms that we mistake for reality, while the sunlight outside the cave symbolizes the higher truth, the world of *Forms* in Plato's philosophy. Just as Yogamaya veils the truth of Brahman, the prisoners in the cave are veiled by the shadows, unable to perceive the true nature of existence. And just as spiritual awakening in Hinduism involves transcending the illusions of Maya, in Platonic philosophy, enlightenment involves turning away from the shadows and seeking the higher reality beyond them.

Christian Mysticism: The Veil of Illusion and Divine Grace

In Christian mysticism, the idea of illusion is often expressed through the metaphor of the "veil" that separates humanity from the direct experience of God. While the terminology differs, the fundamental concept is similar to that of Yogamaya—the world we perceive is not the ultimate reality, and divine grace is required to pierce the veil and attain a direct experience of the divine.

In the Christian tradition, mystics such as *Meister Eckhart* and *St. John of the Cross* speak of the soul's journey toward union with God, a journey that requires the soul to transcend the distractions and illusions of the material world. St. John of the Cross, in his famous work *The Dark Night of the Soul*, describes the process by which the soul is purified through suffering and detachment from worldly desires. This process allows the soul to move beyond the "veil" that obscures the presence of God, leading to a mystical union with the divine.

The Christian idea of the "veil" can be compared to the concept of Maya in Hinduism. Both represent a barrier that separates the individual soul from the ultimate truth, and both can be transcended through spiritual practice, devotion, and the grace of God. In Hinduism, it is through the grace of Yogamaya that one can see through the illusions of the material world and realize the oneness of Brahman. Similarly, in Christian mysticism, it is through divine grace that the soul is able to pierce the veil and experience the presence of God.

Sufism: The Veil of Separation in Islamic Mysticism

In *Sufism*, the mystical branch of Islam, we encounter yet another parallel to Yogamaya in the concept of the *veil of separation* (*hijab*). Sufis speak of the veil as a barrier that prevents the soul from directly experiencing the presence of God (*Allah*). This veil is created by the ego, attachments, and the distractions of the material world, which obscure the divine reality that is always present.

One of the central practices in Sufism is the *dhikr*, or the remembrance of God. Through the constant recitation of God's names and the purification of the heart, the Sufi seeks to lift the veil and attain *fana*—the annihilation of the ego and the merging of the individual soul with the divine. In this state, the Sufi experiences *tawhid*, or the unity of all existence, a realization that mirrors the Hindu concept of *moksha*—the liberation from the illusions of Yogamaya and the realization of oneness with Brahman.

The Sufi mystic *Rumi* often spoke of the veil in his poetry. He described the material world as a distraction that keeps us from experiencing the love of God. In one of his famous verses, he writes:

*"The moment I heard my first love story,
I started looking for you, not knowing
How blind that was.
Lovers don't finally meet somewhere.
They're in each other all along."*

Here, Rumi suggests that the true nature of reality—the love of God—is already present within us, but we are blinded by the veil of illusion. This is remarkably similar to the Hindu understanding of Yogamaya as both the force that conceals and reveals the divine presence.

Modern Philosophy: The Matrix and Simulation Theory

In more recent times, the themes of illusion and reality explored by Yogamaya have found expression in popular culture and modern philosophical thought. One of the most striking examples of this is the 1999 science fiction film *The Matrix*, which presents a dystopian vision of a world where humans live in a simulated reality created by machines. The protagonist, Neo, discovers that the world he thought was real is actually a computer-generated illusion, and he embarks on a journey to awaken from the simulation and discover the truth.

The Matrix has been widely interpreted as an allegory for the spiritual journey, with the simulated reality representing Maya, the illusory world of appearances, and Neo's awakening representing the realization of the deeper truth. In fact, many elements of the film's narrative are drawn from Eastern philosophies, including Hinduism and Buddhism, where the idea of breaking free from illusion and awakening to the truth is central.

In contemporary philosophical discussions, the question of whether we live in a simulation has been taken seriously by thinkers like *Nick Bostrom*, who posits the simulation hypothesis. This thought experiment raises fundamental questions about the nature of reality, perception, and existence—questions that echo the ancient inquiries of philosophers and mystics alike. The notion that our perceived reality may be an illusion resonates deeply with the teachings of Yogamaya, as both challenge us to question the nature of our existence and seek a higher understanding of reality.

Conclusion: A Universal Quest for Truth

These comparisons illuminate the profound and universal nature of the quest for truth that resides at the heart of human existence. Regardless of cultural background, spiritual tradition, or historical context, the exploration of reality and illusion is a common thread that binds humanity together. Whether articulated through the lens of Yogamaya in Hinduism, Maya in Buddhism, the allegory of the cave in Platonic philosophy, or the mystical veils in Christian and Sufi teachings, the struggle to discern the true nature of existence is a shared human experience.

In every tradition, we find a recognition that our perceptions may not encompass the entirety of reality. This acknowledgment of illusion—the shadows on the wall of the cave, the distractions of the material world, the layers of separation from the divine—serves as a call to deeper understanding. Each path offers unique insights and methodologies for transcending these illusions, urging seekers to embark on a transformative journey towards awakening and realization.

Through spiritual practice, contemplation, and the guidance of enlightened beings, individuals are invited to lift the veils that obscure their understanding. The journey involves not only an intellectual pursuit but also a profound inner transformation, wherein the seeker must confront their attachments, fears, and misconceptions. This path to awakening—be it through the grace of Yogamaya, the insights of philosophical thought, or the mystical experiences of various traditions—ultimately leads to the realization of the interconnectedness of all beings and the presence of the divine within.

Moreover, the parallels we have drawn between Yogamaya and other traditions illustrate the importance of dialogue and cross-cultural understanding in our contemporary world. In an era marked by globalization and the sharing of ideas, recognizing the commonalities among different spiritual philosophies can foster greater empathy and appreciation for the diverse expressions of humanity's search for meaning. Instead of viewing these traditions as disparate or conflicting, we can embrace them as complementary paths leading toward the same ultimate truth—a truth that transcends language, doctrine, and dogma.

In conclusion, the exploration of Yogamaya and its resonance with similar concepts across traditions invites us to embark on a universal quest for truth. This quest is not merely an intellectual exercise; it is a profound journey of the heart and spirit. As we seek to understand the illusions that bind us and the deeper realities that lie beyond, we are reminded of the wisdom of the ages: that the pursuit of truth is a journey worth undertaking, one that ultimately leads to liberation, unity, and the realization of our shared humanity.

As we move forward into the subsequent chapters of this exploration, we will delve deeper into the various manifestations of Yogamaya, the narratives that illustrate her power, and the ways in which she can be invoked for personal transformation. The quest for truth continues, and with each revelation, we draw closer to understanding the sacred dance of illusion and reality that shapes our existence. Let us journey together into the heart of Yogamaya, where the divine and the ephemeral intertwine, guiding us toward the ultimate realization of our true selves.

- **The duality of reality: Maya vs. Yogamaya**

In the vast expanse of cosmic existence, where time is endless and space infinite, the ancient seers of India delved into the mysteries of the universe and human perception. They sought to understand not only the nature of the external world but also the inner workings of the human mind, the soul, and the ultimate truth. From their profound explorations arose the concept of duality that shapes our reality: **Maya** and **Yogamaya**.

This duality is not simply an abstract philosophical concept, but the very fabric of existence that weaves through the lives of every individual. To grasp the true essence of this duality, one must first journey through the layers of illusion and truth, appearance and reality, superficiality and depth. It is a journey into the heart of existence itself.

The Birth of Maya: The Veil of Illusion

In the beginning, there was nothing but the infinite, unmanifest consciousness—Brahman, the absolute reality. Beyond time, space, and causality, Brahman exists in a state of pure being, untouched by the material universe. It is pure consciousness, pure bliss, and pure existence. However, the moment Brahman decides to create, a veil is cast over this infinite reality. This veil is known as **Maya**.

Maya is often described as illusion, but it is far more complex than a mere deception. It is the force that creates the world as we perceive it—the material world with its dualities, limitations, and separations. Through the lens of Maya, the One appears as many. Maya divides the indivisible, giving rise to forms, shapes, and names. It creates a world where the eternal appears transient, where unity is experienced as diversity, and where the limitless is seen as bound.

Maya is the reason we perceive ourselves as separate from the divine, separate from nature, and separate from each other. It binds the soul, the **Atman**, to the body and mind, making us believe that we are nothing more than this limited human existence. Our senses, conditioned by Maya, deceive us into thinking that the material world is the only reality.

Imagine a man standing by a serene lake. As he gazes into the water, he sees the reflection of the moon. Enchanted by its beauty, he forgets that the moon is not in the lake but in the sky above. The reflection, while real in its own right, is not the true moon. It is merely an image created by the interplay of light and water. This is Maya—the reflection of the divine reality, which, while enchanting and beautiful, is not the ultimate truth.

Maya is responsible for the **Bhava-Roga**—the disease of worldly existence. It causes attachment, desire, fear, and suffering. It makes us chase after material pleasures and temporary joys, forgetting that true happiness lies beyond the veil. It entangles us in the web of **Samsara**, the endless cycle of birth, death, and rebirth.

Yet, Maya is not inherently evil. It is part of the divine play, the **Leela** of creation. Without Maya, there would be no world, no experience, no life. Maya is the creative power that gives form to the formless, structure to the unstructured. It is both a binding force and a tool for liberation, depending on how one perceives it.

The Dance of Yogamaya: The Power of Divine Illusion

But beyond Maya, there is another force—**Yogamaya**. While Maya binds, confuses, and leads souls away from the ultimate truth, Yogamaya reveals, liberates, and guides the soul back to its divine origin.

Yogamaya is the **divine** version of Maya, the power used by the Lord to perform His divine activities. It is not an illusion in the ordinary sense but a divine illusion, a transcendental energy that hides the true glory of the Lord from the uninitiated while simultaneously revealing it to those who are blessed with divine vision. Yogamaya is the Lord's internal potency, the power through which He manifests His divine pastimes, or **Leelas**, in the world.

Where Maya creates the appearance of multiplicity and separation, Yogamaya reveals the underlying unity of all existence. It is the force through which the Lord manifests His various forms, from the majestic **Vishnu** to the mischievous **Krishna**, and yet remains beyond the grasp of the material mind. Through Yogamaya, the divine chooses to appear in the material world, interacting with it without ever becoming bound by it.

In the great epics and scriptures, Yogamaya plays a pivotal role. For example, in the **Bhagavad Gita**, Lord Krishna speaks to Arjuna about His divine nature, explaining how, though He manifests in the world, He is never tainted by it. This is possible through Yogamaya, the power that allows the divine to engage with the material world while remaining transcendent.

Yogamaya also manifests in the lives of devotees. When a devotee's love for the divine reaches its zenith, Yogamaya lifts the veil of Maya, allowing the devotee to see the divine in all things. This is the state of **Bhakti**, where the world, once seen as a place of suffering and separation, becomes a playground of divine joy. In this state, the devotee no longer sees the world as an illusion but as a manifestation of divine love. Everything becomes sacred, every moment becomes a dance with the divine.

In the story of **Radha and Krishna**, Yogamaya is ever-present. Radha's love for Krishna is not bound by the limitations of the material world. It transcends time, space, and even individuality. Through Yogamaya, Radha experiences union with Krishna, not as a separate entity but as an inseparable part of Him. Their love is not bound by the illusions of Maya but is a divine play, orchestrated by Yogamaya to reveal the highest truth—that of pure, selfless love for the divine.

The Interplay Between Maya and Yogamaya

The distinction between Maya and Yogamaya is subtle yet profound. Maya is the veil that covers the divine truth, making us see the world as fragmented and separate from the divine. It binds the soul to the material world, creating the experience of suffering and limitation. Yogamaya, on the other hand, is the divine power that, while appearing to veil the truth, actually reveals it to those who are ready.

One could think of Maya as the night that covers the landscape in darkness, hiding the beauty of the world. Yogamaya, however, is like the twilight, where the darkness still lingers, but the light of dawn is beginning to break through, revealing the hidden beauty of the world. To the untrained eye, both may seem to obscure the truth, but to those who have the eyes to see, Yogamaya is a blessing, for it prepares the soul for the ultimate revelation.

In spiritual practice, the goal is to transcend the illusions of Maya and come under the shelter of Yogamaya. Through **meditation**, **selfless service**, and **devotion**, the soul gradually pierces the veil of Maya, realizing that the world of appearances is not the ultimate reality. The world, with all its joys and sorrows, is seen for what it is—a temporary manifestation of the divine play.

However, the story does not end with the rejection of the world. Yogamaya leads the soul to the deeper understanding that the world, while not the ultimate reality, is still a sacred manifestation of the divine. It is a stage where the divine drama of life unfolds, a canvas on which the Lord paints His infinite expressions of love, compassion, and beauty.

Maya and Yogamaya in the Modern World

In the modern age, the duality of Maya and Yogamaya is more relevant than ever. We live in a world where materialism, consumerism, and external success are often equated with happiness. The illusion of Maya is strong, leading many to believe that the fulfillment of worldly desires will bring lasting joy. People chase after wealth, power, and fame, only to find themselves trapped in a never-ending cycle of dissatisfaction.

Yet, even in this age of illusion, Yogamaya is at work. Beneath the surface, there is a growing yearning for something deeper, something more meaningful. Spiritual practices, meditation, and a return to inner wisdom are gaining popularity as people seek to pierce the veil of Maya and find the divine reality that lies beyond.

In truth, both Maya and Yogamaya are divine energies, serving the greater purpose of the universe's evolution. Maya teaches the soul through contrast—the contrast of pleasure and pain, attachment and loss, joy and suffering. It is only through experiencing the limitations of Maya that the soul begins to long for something more, something eternal. Yogamaya answers this call, guiding the soul towards liberation, towards the realization that behind the illusion of separation lies the unity of all existence.

Conclusion: Beyond Duality

The duality of Maya and Yogamaya is a reflection of the deeper duality that permeates all of creation—the duality of ignorance and wisdom, bondage and liberation, separation and unity. Yet, at the highest level of realization, even this duality dissolves. Maya and Yogamaya, while appearing as two distinct forces, are ultimately one. They are both manifestations of the divine play, serving the same purpose: to lead the soul back to the ultimate truth, the truth of oneness with the divine.

In the end, the journey through Maya and Yogamaya is the journey of the soul. It is the journey from ignorance to knowledge, from illusion to truth, from bondage to freedom. And in this journey, every step, every experience, is a part of the divine play, a dance with the infinite that leads the soul back to its true home—union with the divine.

- The role of Yogamaya in spiritual evolution

In the grand cosmic narrative, where the infinite and the finite intertwine, where light dances with shadow, and where the soul embarks on an eternal quest for truth, there is one force—**Yogamaya**—that plays an extraordinary role. It is not just a mystical energy that influences reality; it is the key to understanding the highest purpose of life, the essence of spiritual evolution. To understand Yogamaya is to uncover the secret thread that connects the soul with the divine, the worldly with the transcendent.

This chapter embarks on an epic exploration of Yogamaya's role in guiding the soul from the depths of ignorance to the heights of enlightenment. It is a journey through the veils of illusion, through time, space, and the limitations of the material world, into the realm of transcendental truth.

The Cosmic Play: The Stage Set by Yogamaya

In the beginning, the universe was an unfathomable sea of undifferentiated consciousness. There were no stars, no planets, no living beings—only the infinite potential of **Brahman**, the absolute. In this eternal silence, the divine willed the creation of the cosmos. From this supreme consciousness, an impulse emerged—the desire to manifest.

To bring forth creation, Brahman needed a force to bridge the gap between the unmanifest and the manifest, between the infinite and the finite. That force was **Yogamaya**.

Yogamaya, the divine power of illusion, is not an illusion in the ordinary sense. Unlike **Maya**, which binds and deludes the individual soul, Yogamaya is the supreme energy that orchestrates the divine play, or **Leela**. It is the creative energy through which the divine projects itself into the world, while simultaneously remaining untouched by it. Through Yogamaya, the infinite Brahman takes on various forms, enters into relationships with its own creation, and yet remains transcendent, beyond the limitations of time and space.

Imagine a vast cosmic stage, where every soul is an actor, each playing a unique role in the grand drama of existence. Yogamaya is the director of this cosmic theater, ensuring that every role, every scene, every event unfolds perfectly. But unlike a mere director, Yogamaya is also the scriptwriter, the choreographer, and the set designer. Through Yogamaya, the divine manifests the universe with all its intricacies, from the swirling galaxies to the blossoming flowers, from the rise and fall of civilizations to the silent meditation of a lone monk.

However, Yogamaya's role does not stop at creation. Its true power lies in guiding the souls on their spiritual journey, leading them through the labyrinth of worldly existence toward the ultimate truth of unity with the divine.

The Soul's Descent into Ignorance

At the heart of spiritual evolution is the journey of the soul, or **Atman**, which is an eternal spark of the divine. In its original state, the soul is pure, luminous, and united with the supreme consciousness. It is a part of the divine, without beginning or end. But when the soul takes birth in the material world, it becomes covered by the layers of **Maya**, the energy of illusion that veils its true nature.

Maya causes the soul to forget its divine origin. It identifies itself with the body, the mind, and the material world. Caught in the web of desires, attachments, and aversions, the soul becomes entangled in **Samsara**, the endless cycle of birth, death, and rebirth. This cycle, driven by ignorance, is the root of all suffering.

It is here, in the thick of this spiritual darkness, that Yogamaya plays its most crucial role. While Maya binds the soul to the world of illusion, Yogamaya works silently behind the scenes, creating opportunities for the soul to remember its true nature. The divine, in its infinite compassion, does not leave the soul in perpetual bondage. Through Yogamaya, it constantly calls the soul back, offering glimpses of the higher reality, drawing the soul closer to liberation.

The Awakening: Yogamaya's Gentle Nudge

The journey of spiritual evolution is not a straight path. It is marked by countless twists and turns, moments of profound insight followed by periods of confusion and doubt. Yogamaya, as the guiding force, ensures that every experience, whether joyful or painful, serves a higher purpose.

Imagine a traveler walking through a dense forest. The path is overgrown, and the destination is hidden from view. Along the way, the traveler encounters various obstacles—thorns, wild animals, and deceptive trails. But every now and then, a gentle breeze blows, parting the branches and revealing a brief glimpse of the distant mountain peak. These glimpses, fleeting though they may be, remind the traveler of the goal and give them the strength to continue.

Yogamaya acts like that gentle breeze. It orchestrates moments of awakening, moments where the soul, despite being entangled in the world, experiences flashes of higher truth. These moments can come in the form of a profound spiritual experience, a sudden insight during meditation, or even through the love and compassion of another person. They serve as reminders that the material world is not the ultimate reality, that there is something higher, something eternal waiting to be realized.

For the average person, these moments might seem like coincidences, but for the soul on the path of spiritual evolution, they are divine interventions. Yogamaya is constantly at work, arranging circumstances, people, and events in such a way that the soul is gradually led toward liberation.

Yogamaya and the Path of Devotion

In the great spiritual traditions of India, especially in the path of **Bhakti** (devotion), Yogamaya plays an especially intimate role. Bhakti is the path of love for the divine, where the soul seeks union not through intellectual understanding or austere practices, but through the surrender of the heart.

The stories of **Krishna** and **Radha**, of **Rama** and **Hanuman**, and the countless tales of saints and devotees, all point to the power of Yogamaya in Bhakti. In these stories, Yogamaya manifests as the divine play, allowing the Lord to appear in human form and interact with His devotees. Through Yogamaya, the Lord hides His true nature, appearing as a child, a lover, or a friend, and engages in the most intimate relationships with His devotees.

Take the example of the **Gopis** of Vrindavan, who are considered the greatest devotees of Lord Krishna. For them, Krishna was not the supreme Lord of the universe, but their beloved friend, their lover, their everything. They were completely unaware of His divine nature, and yet, through their love, they attained the highest realization. This was possible only through the grace of Yogamaya.

Yogamaya veils the divine's supreme majesty so that the devotee can love the Lord in the most personal way. If the Gopis had known that Krishna was the omnipotent, omniscient Lord, their love would have been tinged with awe and reverence. But through the influence of Yogamaya, they were able to love Him purely, without any sense of separation or difference.

In the path of Bhakti, Yogamaya thus acts as the mediator between the soul and the divine, allowing the soul to experience the highest love while slowly revealing the truth of the divine's supreme nature.

The Gradual Unveiling: Yogamaya and Liberation

As the soul progresses on the path of spiritual evolution, Yogamaya gradually lifts the veil of illusion. The more the soul surrenders to the divine, the more it sees through the illusions of the material world. The once all-encompassing attachments, desires, and fears begin to lose their hold. The soul starts to experience a deep sense of peace and contentment, no longer swayed by the fluctuations of worldly life.

But Yogamaya's role is not simply to remove the illusions of Maya. It also prepares the soul for the ultimate realization—that the divine is not separate from the world, but present in every atom of existence. This realization, known as **Advaita** or non-duality, is the pinnacle of spiritual evolution.

Yogamaya reveals that the world, while appearing to be a place of suffering and bondage, is actually the divine play of consciousness. Every experience, every interaction, every moment of life is a manifestation of the divine. The soul, which once felt isolated and separate from the world, realizes that it is one with all of creation, one with the divine.

This final unveiling is the culmination of Yogamaya's work. It is the moment of **Moksha**, or liberation, where the soul transcends the cycle of birth and death and merges back into the infinite ocean of Brahman. But even in this state of liberation, Yogamaya continues to play its role, ensuring that the liberated soul remains engaged in the world, not out of attachment, but out of compassion for all beings still trapped in the illusions of Maya.

The Endless Journey: Yogamaya's Eternal Role

Even after the soul attains liberation, Yogamaya's role is far from over. Spiritual evolution is not a linear journey with a final endpoint. It is an ever-deepening spiral, where the soul continues to experience new layers of the divine mystery.

Yogamaya, in its infinite wisdom, keeps the soul engaged in the dance of creation, not as a prisoner of illusion, but as a participant in the divine play. The liberated soul, while free from ignorance and bondage, chooses to remain in the world out of love and compassion, helping other souls awaken to their true nature.

In this way, Yogamaya ensures the continuity of the cosmic drama. It allows the divine to express itself in infinite forms, while simultaneously guiding each soul toward the ultimate realization of unity. Yogamaya is both the force that creates the illusion of separation and the force that dissolves it, revealing the eternal truth of oneness.

Conclusion: Yogamaya as the Supreme Guide

The role of Yogamaya in spiritual evolution is both profound and all-encompassing. It is the invisible hand that guides the soul through the maze of worldly existence, providing glimpses of truth, arranging moments of awakening, and ultimately leading the soul to liberation.

Without Yogamaya, the journey of the soul would be impossible. It is the divine energy that bridges the gap between the material and the spiritual, between the finite and the infinite. Through Yogamaya, the soul comes to realize that the world, with all its joys and sorrows, is not a prison, but a stage for the divine play—a play in which every soul is both an actor and the audience, eternally participating in the dance of creation.

Yogamaya is the ultimate guide on the path of spiritual evolution, the force that ensures that every soul, no matter how lost it may seem, will eventually return to the source of all existence, to the infinite ocean of divine consciousness. And in this return, the soul will realize that the journey itself was the goal, that every step was a part of the divine dance, orchestrated by the loving hand of Yogamaya.

Chapter 2: The Nature of Illusion

- Defining illusion in spiritual terms

Illusion—Maya—is one of the most profound concepts in spirituality, intricately woven into the fabric of human existence and the universe itself. Its subtle yet pervasive nature shapes the way we perceive reality and influences our actions, thoughts, and desires. To truly grasp the depth of illusion is to embark on a journey of self-discovery, as it reveals not only the illusory nature of the world around us but also the veils that shroud our inner consciousness. The nature of illusion goes beyond mere deception or trickery; it encompasses the very foundations of perception, consciousness, and the eternal dance between the seen and the unseen.

In spiritual terms, illusion is often referred to as **Maya**, a Sanskrit word that holds within it layers of meaning. Maya is not just about falseness; it is the principle that governs the world of appearances and duality. To understand illusion, we must first acknowledge the dichotomy between the *real* and the *unreal*, between the eternal and the transient, between the absolute truth and the shifting forms of existence.

The Dance of Maya: Illusion and Reality

Maya, the cosmic illusion, operates on both the macrocosmic and microcosmic levels. At the level of the universe, Maya creates the phenomenal world—the world of names and forms. Everything that we experience with our senses, everything we believe to be solid, real, and lasting, is under the spell of Maya. It is Maya that gives form to formlessness, structure to the unstructured, and multiplicity to the One. The world, as we perceive it, is a complex web of interactions between matter, time, and space, all of which are manifestations of Maya.

In Hindu philosophy, it is said that **Brahman**, the ultimate reality, is the only truth. Brahman is formless, infinite, and eternal, beyond the grasp of the senses and the mind. However, when Brahman interacts with Maya, it appears as the world of multiplicity—the world that we see and experience every day. This world, although seemingly real, is subject to constant change, decay, and death. In this sense, it is illusory, because it lacks the permanence and stability of the true, underlying reality.

Just as a skilled magician creates an elaborate illusion, captivating the audience and making them believe in the impossible, Maya weaves a web around our consciousness, making us believe that the material world is the ultimate reality. But just as an illusion dissolves the moment the trick is revealed, so too does Maya lose its hold the moment we realize the truth of Brahman.

Perception: The First Step into Illusion

From the moment we are born, we are caught in the web of perception. The world presents itself to us through the senses—sight, sound, touch, taste, and smell. These senses are our primary tools for interacting with the external world, yet they are also the first gatekeepers of illusion. The mind processes these sensory inputs and constructs a reality that is based on subjective experience. Two individuals can look at the same object, yet perceive it in entirely different ways. What one person finds beautiful, another may find ugly. What one finds joyful, another may find sorrowful. These differences arise because our minds interpret the world through the filters of past experiences, emotions, and desires, creating a personal version of reality.

However, this reality is not the ultimate truth—it is a reflection, a shadow of the higher truth that exists beyond the senses. The ancient Vedic sages often compared the mind to a mirror. When the mirror is clear and free of dust, it reflects the truth accurately. But when it is covered in layers of dust—representing desires, attachments, and ignorance—it distorts the reflection. The more we cling to our perceptions, the more deeply we become entangled in illusion.

The Ego: The Architect of Illusion

At the heart of illusion lies the ego, the sense of individuality that separates us from the whole. The ego creates the illusion of separateness, making us believe that we are distinct beings, independent from the rest of creation. This sense of separation gives rise to the dualities that dominate our existence—pleasure and pain, success and failure, life and death. The ego is constantly seeking to affirm itself, to validate its existence by attaching itself to the fleeting things of the world—wealth, power, fame, relationships, and even spiritual achievements.

However, all of these things are subject to change, and when they inevitably fade or slip away, the ego suffers. This suffering, according to spiritual teachings, arises from ignorance—the ignorance of our true nature. The ego, in its delusion, believes that it is the doer, the controller, and the enjoyer, when in reality, it is merely a temporary construct, a mask worn by the soul during its journey through the material world.

To break free from the illusion of the ego is one of the central goals of spiritual practice. This process is often likened to waking up from a dream. Just as we realize upon waking that the events of the dream were not real, so too do we awaken to the truth that the ego, and the world it clings to, are part of the great illusion of Maya.

Time: The Eternal Trickster

Another aspect of illusion is the concept of time. Time, as we perceive it, is linear—we believe that the past is behind us, the present is now, and the future is yet to come. This linear perception of time is a product of Maya. In the ultimate reality of Brahman, time does not exist as we know it. Brahman is beyond time, existing in an eternal now, where past, present, and future are one.

Yet, in the world of illusion, time is one of the most powerful forces shaping our experience. It gives rise to the cycle of birth, growth, decay, and death—the cycle of **Samsara**. Time creates the illusion of change, making us believe that we are progressing through life, moving towards a future goal. But in truth, we are already complete. The soul is timeless, eternal, and untouched by the ravages of time. The idea that we need to achieve something in the future to be whole is another layer of illusion, perpetuated by the ego.

The Illusion of Desire

Desire is one of the key driving forces behind the experience of illusion. Our desires shape our perceptions and actions, creating attachments to the things we believe will bring us happiness. But these objects of desire—whether material wealth, relationships, or even spiritual experiences—are themselves impermanent, and thus cannot provide lasting fulfillment. When we attach ourselves to these fleeting things, we set ourselves up for disappointment and suffering.

In the Bhagavad Gita, Lord Krishna explains that desire, when left unchecked, leads to anger, confusion, and ultimately, the downfall of the soul. It is desire that binds us to the wheel of Samsara, the cycle of birth and rebirth. Yet, like all things in the world of Maya, desire itself is illusory. The fulfillment we seek outside of ourselves already exists within us, but the veil of illusion prevents us from seeing it.

Liberation from Maya: The Path of Wisdom

While Maya is powerful and all-encompassing, it is not invincible. The ancient spiritual texts speak of liberation—**Moksha**—as the ultimate goal of human life. Moksha is the state of freedom from the cycle of birth and death, the transcendence of Maya, and the realization of the true nature of the Self as Brahman. This liberation comes through the cultivation of wisdom—**Jnana**.

The process of dispelling illusion is not an easy one. It requires deep introspection, self-discipline, and the guidance of a teacher. The spiritual path often involves practices such as meditation, self-inquiry, and detachment from worldly desires. By turning inward and focusing on the higher truth, we begin to peel away the layers of illusion, much like peeling the layers of an onion, revealing the core of our true existence.

The great sages have often emphasized the importance of **discrimination**—the ability to distinguish between the real and the unreal, the eternal and the transient. This practice, known as **Viveka**, is essential in the pursuit of truth. Through Viveka, we learn to see beyond the surface appearances of the world, recognizing the illusory nature of material existence, and focusing our attention on the unchanging, eternal reality of Brahman.

The Role of Devotion: Bhakti as a Tool for Seeing Through Illusion

While wisdom is a powerful tool for breaking free from illusion, the path of **Bhakti**, or devotion, offers another means of transcending Maya. Through sincere devotion to the Divine, one can cultivate a sense of surrender, letting go of the ego and its attachments. In Bhakti, the devotee seeks to dissolve the sense of individuality, merging with the divine will, and thus, transcending the illusions of the world.

Bhakti allows the heart to see what the mind cannot comprehend. When one is immersed in love for the Divine, the veils of illusion begin to lift naturally, revealing the underlying truth of existence.

Conclusion: The Journey Beyond Illusion

The nature of illusion is complex and multifaceted, touching every aspect of human experience. From the perception of the external world to the internal workings of the mind, Maya shapes the way we see and interact with reality. Yet, it is not a force to be feared, but a challenge to be understood and transcended.

Breaking free from illusion is not a one-time event, but a lifelong process. It requires a deep commitment to truth, a willingness to question our assumptions, and the courage to face the unknown. But once the veil of illusion is lifted, even momentarily, the experience of reality is transformed. What was once seen as separate, fragmented, and fleeting becomes whole, eternal, and unified.

In the end, the journey through illusion is not about escaping the world, but about seeing it for what it truly is—a reflection of the divine, a dance of consciousness, where every moment holds the potential for awakening.

- **How perceptions shape our reality**

In the dim recesses of the human mind lies a force more potent than any external influence, more transformative than the most advanced technology, and more profound than the deepest philosophies. This force, quietly at work within every moment of existence, determines the world we experience and how we move through it. It is the unseen architect of our joys and sorrows, our beliefs and actions—**perception**.

Perception is the lens through which we view reality, the invisible filter that colors every experience. But perception is not simply a passive reception of sensory data; it is an active, dynamic process. It shapes, bends, and often distorts reality according to our thoughts, emotions, memories, and desires. To understand how perceptions shape our reality is to unlock the key to our entire experience of life. It is to see how the stories we tell ourselves about the world become the world we live in.

In this chapter, we will journey through the intricate landscape of perception, exploring how it is formed, how it functions, and how it ultimately creates the reality each of us experiences. We will uncover how perception, though subjective and fluid, can become a powerful tool for transformation, allowing us to reshape our world by changing the way we see it.

The Human Mind: The Alchemist of Reality

Imagine waking up one morning in a fog-covered valley. The air is thick with mist, and the shapes of trees, mountains, and houses are blurred and indistinct. You step outside and feel disoriented. Your familiar surroundings are suddenly unfamiliar, altered by the haze that covers everything. Now imagine that same valley an hour later when the fog lifts. The world you know re-emerges, clear and distinct. The mountains, the trees, the houses—they haven't changed. What changed was your perception of them.

This fog is like the mind. It doesn't simply show us the world as it is. Instead, it acts like a veil, obscuring, distorting, and sometimes completely altering our experience of reality. But unlike the fog that eventually clears on its own, the mind's veil is often self-created and persistent. It is woven from past experiences, beliefs, cultural conditioning, and emotions. These elements combine to form a unique lens through which each individual sees the world.

Two people standing side by side may look at the same sunset, but their perceptions will be vastly different. One might be awestruck by the beauty of the colors blending into the horizon, feeling a deep sense of peace and wonder. The other might feel indifferent, preoccupied with a troubling memory, barely noticing the sunset at all. The reality is the same—the sun is setting—but the experience of that reality is entirely different.

This is the alchemy of perception. It takes raw sensory input—the colors, sounds, smells, and textures of the world—and transforms it into personal meaning. The world we see, the world we live in, is not an objective reality but a subjective interpretation shaped by our mind.

The Illusions of Perception

Throughout history, philosophers and spiritual teachers have suggested that the world we perceive is not the ultimate reality but a construct of the mind. The ancient Indian seers spoke of **Maya**, the illusion that veils the true nature of reality. In more modern times, thinkers like **Immanuel Kant** suggested that we can never know the world "as it is," only the world as we perceive it through the filter of our senses and cognition.

But the mind is not an impartial observer. It is shaped by countless influences—genetics, upbringing, education, culture, and personal experiences. These influences form mental frameworks or **schemas**, through which we interpret the world. These schemas determine how we respond to new situations, how we judge others, and how we understand ourselves. They shape not only our thoughts but also our emotions, behaviors, and decisions.

Take the example of a child who grows up in a household where failure is harshly criticized. As this child grows, their mind develops a schema around the concept of failure—it becomes associated with shame, inadequacy, and rejection. As an adult, this person might avoid taking risks or trying new things, not because failure itself is a catastrophic event, but because their perception of failure is colored by their early experiences. The reality of failure hasn't changed—it remains a natural part of life—but their perception of it creates a reality in which failure is something to be feared and avoided at all costs.

Perception also creates **cognitive distortions**, where reality is bent to fit our emotional state. When we are feeling anxious, for example, our perception of the world narrows. Every interaction seems fraught with danger, every decision feels overwhelming, and every outcome is seen in terms of worst-case scenarios. The world becomes a reflection of our internal state, a mirror of our fears.

In the same way, when we are in love, the world seems brighter, more beautiful, and full of possibilities. The person we love appears flawless, their every word and gesture imbued with meaning. This is not because the external world has changed, but because our perception of it has shifted.

Perception and Reality: The Observer Effect

To understand the power of perception fully, we can turn to a surprising source: quantum physics. In the strange and often counterintuitive world of quantum mechanics, there is a concept known as the **observer effect**. This principle suggests that the act of observing something can change its behavior. At the subatomic level, particles exist in a state of probability—they can be in multiple places or states at once. But when an observer measures or observes them, these particles collapse into a single state.

In a metaphorical sense, this is how perception works. Our act of observing reality—our attention, thoughts, and interpretations—collapses the infinite possibilities of the world into a specific experience. The world is not a fixed, unchanging entity. It is fluid, malleable, and influenced by how we perceive it.

This means that reality is not something "out there," separate from us. We are active participants in the creation of our reality. The thoughts we think, the beliefs we hold, and the emotions we feel all contribute to the world we experience. By changing our perceptions, we can change our reality.

The Role of Belief Systems in Shaping Perception

At the heart of perception are our **beliefs**. These deeply ingrained ideas about ourselves, others, and the world form the foundation of how we interpret reality. Beliefs act like filters, allowing in information that supports them while rejecting or distorting information that contradicts them.

For example, someone who believes that people are generally untrustworthy will interpret interactions with others through this lens. They may notice subtle cues—like a pause before answering a question or a lack of eye contact—and perceive these as signs of dishonesty. Over time, this perception reinforces their belief, creating a self-fulfilling cycle. The person's belief shapes their perception, and their perception, in turn, reinforces their belief.

In contrast, someone who believes in the goodness of people will interpret the same interaction in a completely different way. A pause in conversation may be seen as thoughtfulness, and lack of eye contact as a sign of shyness rather than deception. This person's belief leads to a perception of the world as a generally safe and trustworthy place.

This is the power of belief. It not only shapes how we see the world but also how the world responds to us. Our beliefs act like magnets, attracting experiences that confirm them and repelling experiences that contradict them. This is why changing deeply held beliefs can be so transformative—it can fundamentally alter our reality.

Emotions and the Lens of Perception

While beliefs are the foundation of perception, emotions are the driving force that colors it. Emotions act like magnifying glasses, intensifying our perceptions and often distorting them in the process.

When we are angry, for example, our perception of the world becomes narrow and focused on the object of our anger. Minor annoyances become major offenses, and we interpret neutral or even positive actions as hostile. Our emotional state alters our perception, making the world seem more threatening or unjust than it really is.

Conversely, when we are joyful, our perception expands. We become more open to others, more willing to see the good in situations, and more inclined to interpret events in a positive light. The world seems brighter, friendlier, and full of possibilities.

Emotions not only affect how we perceive the world in the moment but also how we remember and interpret past events. Studies in psychology show that our memories are highly influenced by our emotional state at the time of the event, as well as when we recall it. A memory of a past argument may feel more intense and painful when we are in a bad mood, while the same memory may seem trivial when we are feeling happy.

In this way, emotions create a feedback loop that shapes our reality. The way we feel affects how we perceive the world, and how we perceive the world affects how we feel. By learning to manage and understand our emotions, we can gain greater control over how we experience reality.

The Role of Perception in Relationships

Perception doesn't just shape our internal world—it plays a crucial role in our relationships with others. Every interaction we have is filtered through our perceptions of the other person, as well as our perceptions of ourselves. These perceptions, often based on incomplete or biased information, can create misunderstandings, conflicts, and even deep rifts in relationships.

Take, for example, a couple arguing about a trivial issue—perhaps one partner left the dishes unwashed. To one partner, this may be a minor oversight, but to the other, it may be perceived as a sign of disrespect or carelessness. The reality of the situation is the same—the dishes were left unwashed—but each person's perception of the event is different, shaped by their past experiences, emotions, and beliefs.

If the partner who feels disrespected has a belief that they are often taken for granted, they may interpret this small event as confirmation of that belief. Their perception of the situation is not just about the dishes—it is colored by a deeper narrative about their relationship and their own self-worth.

In this way, perception creates a kind of reality within relationships. We see others not as they truly are, but as we believe them to be. Our expectations, fears, and desires all shape our perception of the other person, often leading to distorted views and misunderstandings.

The challenge in relationships is to recognize that our perceptions are not always accurate reflections of reality. By becoming aware of our own perceptual biases and actively working to see others more clearly, we can improve communication, deepen understanding, and foster greater harmony in our relationships.

The Transformative Power of Shifting Perception

Given the immense power that perception holds over our reality, it is worth asking: Can we change our perception? And if so, can changing our perception change our life?

The answer is a resounding **yes**. While our perceptions are often deeply ingrained, they are not fixed. By becoming aware of the ways in which our perceptions shape our reality, we can begin to consciously shift them. This process is at the heart of many spiritual and psychological practices, from mindfulness and meditation to cognitive-behavioral therapy and positive psychology.

Take mindfulness, for example. This ancient practice teaches us to observe our thoughts and perceptions without judgment, allowing us to see them for what they are—temporary, subjective experiences. By practicing mindfulness, we can begin to break the automatic link between perception and reaction. We can create space between the stimulus (what happens to us) and our perception of that stimulus, allowing for a more balanced and clear response.

Similarly, cognitive-behavioral therapy (CBT) helps individuals recognize and challenge distorted perceptions, replacing them with more balanced and realistic ones. By changing the way we perceive situations, we can change how we feel and, ultimately, how we act.

At a deeper level, spiritual traditions teach that by changing our perception, we can transcend the limitations of the ego and experience a greater sense of unity with the world. In **Advaita Vedanta**, for example, the ultimate goal is to perceive the world not as a collection of separate, individual entities but as an expression of the one, undivided consciousness. This shift in perception is said to lead to liberation, where the individual no longer feels bound by the limitations of the material world.

Conclusion: Perception as the Creator of Reality

Perception is the invisible force that shapes our reality. It is the filter through which we experience the world, and it determines not only what we see but also how we feel, think, and act. Our perceptions are not objective reflections of reality; they are subjective interpretations shaped by our beliefs, emotions, and past experiences.

By becoming aware of the power of perception, we can begin to take control of how we experience the world. We can challenge distorted perceptions, open ourselves to new perspectives, and ultimately reshape our reality. The world we see is not set in stone; it is a reflection of our inner world. By changing how we perceive, we can change how we live.

In this way, perception is both the key and the doorway to a deeper understanding of ourselves and the universe. Through perception, we create our reality. And through conscious awareness, we can transform it.

- **The impact of societal conditioning on individual beliefs**

In every human life, there is a story quietly unfolding beneath the surface—a story of how our beliefs, values, and sense of self are shaped by forces that we may not even realize are at work. These forces, like invisible threads, weave through the fabric of our lives, influencing our thoughts, emotions, decisions, and even our sense of identity. This phenomenon, known as **societal conditioning**, is one of the most powerful yet subtle influences on our beliefs and behavior. It is the process by which individuals, from the moment of birth, are taught, shaped, and molded by the expectations, norms, and values of the society they are born into.

This conditioning can be so pervasive that it often feels like the natural way of life—like gravity or the rising of the sun. Yet, hidden within this process are deep and profound impacts on the individual, influencing everything from how we view ourselves to how we interpret the world. It is the force that determines our ideas of success and failure, our notions of right and wrong, and even the very meaning of happiness. Understanding societal conditioning is key to understanding the very core of who we are.

In this chapter, we will explore the intricate ways in which societal conditioning shapes individual beliefs. We will journey through the layers of culture, family, education, media, and religion to see how they combine to create the world we see, the choices we make, and the people we become. It is a story of invisible influence, but it is also a story of awakening—of how awareness of this conditioning can lead to personal freedom and transformation.

The Early Seeds: Family as the First Society

From the moment we are born, we enter a world of influences that begin to shape our understanding of reality. The family is the first society we encounter, and it is within the family that the earliest seeds of our beliefs are planted. We are born as blank slates, but we quickly begin to absorb the spoken and unspoken lessons of our immediate environment. These early lessons lay the foundation for much of what we come to believe later in life.

Imagine a child growing up in a household where certain values are emphasized: hard work, obedience, and loyalty to tradition. These values become the lens through which the child learns to interpret the world. The child may learn that success is measured by material achievement, that questioning authority is wrong, and that deviating from family norms leads to conflict. These beliefs are not consciously chosen by the child; they are absorbed through everyday interactions and reinforced by the expectations of the family.

Conversely, a child growing up in a household that values creativity, open-mindedness, and questioning of norms may develop a very different set of beliefs. For this child, success might be defined not by external accomplishments but by self-expression and personal fulfillment. Here, the conditioning creates an entirely different framework for understanding the world.

In both cases, the child's beliefs are shaped by the family's values, traditions, and behaviors. These early influences are so profound because, as children, we are impressionable and dependent on the family for survival, love, and a sense of belonging. Family beliefs become our beliefs, often without us even realizing it. These early patterns can be deeply ingrained and hard to shake, even as we grow older and encounter new influences.

Cultural Norms: The Broader Societal Framework

As we grow beyond the immediate sphere of the family, we enter into the larger society with its own set of rules, expectations, and norms. Culture plays a massive role in shaping individual beliefs, providing a framework for what is considered acceptable, valuable, and meaningful. Culture is like a vast, invisible hand that guides our actions, influencing everything from the clothes we wear and the food we eat to the careers we pursue and the relationships we form.

Consider the cultural conditioning around gender roles. In many societies, there are long-standing norms about what is considered "masculine" and "feminine." Boys are often taught to be strong, assertive, and independent, while girls are encouraged to be nurturing, gentle, and cooperative. These gender roles are not biologically determined but are societal constructs that shape individual identities and behavior. From a young age, children are conditioned to fit into these roles, and they learn to align their beliefs and behaviors with societal expectations.

This conditioning extends to nearly every aspect of life. For example, in some cultures, the pursuit of education and a high-paying career is seen as the pinnacle of success, while in others, success may be defined by one's contribution to the community or family. In some societies, material wealth is the ultimate goal, while in others, spiritual fulfillment or inner peace is considered more valuable.

These cultural norms are reinforced by institutions such as schools, religious organizations, and governments, which uphold and transmit the values of the culture. As individuals, we internalize these norms and come to believe that they are "just the way things are." We may never question them because they seem so natural and self-evident. Yet, beneath the surface, these norms shape our beliefs, often limiting our sense of what is possible.

Education: The Systematic Shaping of Beliefs

Formal education is one of the most powerful tools of societal conditioning. From the time we enter school, we are subjected to a system designed not only to impart knowledge but also to shape our values, behaviors, and beliefs. The structure of the education system, the subjects taught, and even the methods of teaching all serve to reinforce the dominant ideologies of the society in which we live.

Schools are not neutral spaces. They are institutions designed to produce individuals who can function within a particular social, political, and economic system. Through education, we learn not only facts and figures but also how to think, what to value, and how to behave. We are taught the history of our country, often from a perspective that reinforces national pride and loyalty. We are taught the importance of hard work, obedience, and competition—values that are essential in a capitalist economy.

At the same time, education can also limit our beliefs by narrowing the range of perspectives we are exposed to. In many cases, alternative viewpoints—whether they be political, social, or philosophical—are marginalized or omitted altogether. For example, in a society that values individualism, collective approaches to problem-solving or communal living may be downplayed or dismissed. In a society that prioritizes economic growth, the environmental or social costs of such growth may not be fully explored in the classroom.

This selective transmission of knowledge shapes our beliefs about what is important, what is true, and what is possible. By the time we graduate from school, many of our beliefs about the world have been firmly established, and we may not even realize that they are the product of a specific system of conditioning.

The Media: The Constant Reinforcement of Beliefs

In the modern world, the media—whether it be television, movies, social media, or advertising—plays a central role in reinforcing societal conditioning. From a young age, we are bombarded with messages about what is desirable, what is acceptable, and what is normal. These messages come at us from all angles, shaping our beliefs in subtle and not-so-subtle ways.

Consider how beauty standards are shaped by the media. Through constant exposure to images of idealized beauty—whether it be the slim, youthful figure of a fashion model or the muscular physique of an action hero—we are conditioned to believe that certain physical attributes are more valuable than others. This conditioning can lead to a host of issues, from body image disorders to self-esteem problems, as individuals try to conform to these often unattainable standards.

The media also plays a significant role in shaping our beliefs about success, happiness, and fulfillment. In countless advertisements, we are sold the idea that happiness comes from consumption—whether it be through buying the latest car, wearing the trendiest clothes, or achieving a certain lifestyle. These messages create a set of beliefs about what it means to live a good life, often promoting materialism and consumerism as the ultimate goals.

At the same time, the media can reinforce stereotypes and biases, perpetuating harmful beliefs about race, gender, class, and other social categories. Through the repeated portrayal of certain groups in specific roles—such as the "angry black man," the "submissive woman," or the "lazy immigrant"—the media shapes our beliefs about these groups and reinforces societal divisions. These beliefs, once internalized, can be difficult to challenge, as they become embedded in our subconscious.

Religion and Spirituality: The Shaping of Beliefs About Existence

Religion and spirituality are among the oldest and most powerful forms of societal conditioning. Throughout history, religious institutions have played a central role in shaping individual beliefs about morality, the nature of existence, and the meaning of life. For many people, religious teachings form the core of their belief system, influencing everything from their daily behaviors to their understanding of the afterlife.

Religious conditioning begins at a young age, often within the family. Children are taught religious doctrines, practices, and rituals that form the foundation of their belief systems. These teachings are reinforced through participation in religious communities, where social pressure and communal reinforcement play a significant role in shaping individual beliefs.

Religious beliefs often provide a framework for understanding life's most fundamental questions: What is the purpose of life? What happens after death? How should we live our lives? For many, these beliefs offer comfort, guidance, and a sense of belonging. However, religious conditioning can also limit individual beliefs by imposing strict rules and dogmas that discourage questioning or alternative viewpoints.

In some cases, religious conditioning can lead to intolerance or division, as individuals come to believe that their faith is the only "true" way of understanding the world. This can create a sense of "us versus them," where those who do not share the same beliefs are seen as outsiders or even enemies. These beliefs, once ingrained, can be difficult to challenge, as they are often tied to deeply held emotions and identities.

Breaking Free: The Power of Awareness and Individual Choice

While societal conditioning exerts a powerful influence on individual beliefs, it is not an inescapable force. One of the greatest gifts of human consciousness is the ability to become aware of the forces shaping our beliefs and to make conscious choices about how we wish to live. Awareness is the first step toward freedom from societal conditioning.

By examining our beliefs and asking where they come from—whether it be from our family, culture, education, or religion—we can begin to see which beliefs truly serve us and which ones may be limiting our potential. This process of self-examination can be challenging, as it often requires us to confront deeply held assumptions and question the very foundations of our identity. However, it is also a liberating process, as it allows us to reclaim our power and choose beliefs that align with our true selves.

In the end, societal conditioning is a part of the human experience, but it does not have to define us. By becoming aware of its influence, we can transcend the limitations it imposes and create a life that is truly our own. The journey toward personal freedom is a lifelong process, but it is one that leads to a deeper understanding of who we are and what we are capable of becoming.

Chapter 3: The Layers of Reality

- **The physical vs. metaphysical dimensions**

There is a story, an ancient one, told in many cultures across time. It is a story of a seeker, someone like you or me, who begins to question the nature of reality. On the surface, life seems simple enough: there is the world we see, touch, and experience—the physical realm—and then there are the thoughts and emotions that stir within us. But beneath the veneer of this familiar world, there exists a deeper, more mysterious dimension that the seeker begins to sense. It is a realm not bound by physical laws, a place where time and space dissolve, and the very fabric of reality reveals itself as infinitely layered. It is the metaphysical dimension, and it has called to seekers for millennia, beckoning them to uncover its mysteries.

This is the story of the **physical vs. metaphysical dimensions**, two worlds that are seemingly separate, yet inextricably linked. One governs the tangible experiences of our daily lives, the other holds the keys to understanding the profound truths of existence. But to understand these layers of reality, we must first unravel what each dimension represents, how they interact, and how exploring these realms leads us to a deeper understanding of ourselves and the universe.

The Physical Dimension: The Realm of Matter and Form

Let us begin with the world we know best—the physical dimension. It is the realm of matter, form, and the five senses. This is the world we navigate daily, the world where our bodies move through space and time, and where cause and effect govern the unfolding of events. It is the world that science seeks to understand through observation, experimentation, and the measurement of objective reality.

From the moment we are born, we are introduced to this physical world. As infants, we reach for objects, attracted to their color, texture, and shape. We learn the laws of gravity by watching a ball fall to the ground, and we experience the boundaries of our own bodies as we crawl, walk, and explore. Over time, we become increasingly familiar with this realm, trusting in its solidity and predictability. The physical dimension is where we eat, sleep, work, and engage in all the activities that make up the human experience.

But while the physical world appears solid and unchanging, science tells us otherwise. Quantum physics, the most advanced exploration of the physical realm, has revealed that what we perceive as solid objects are, in fact, composed of vast amounts of empty space. At the subatomic level, particles flicker in and out of existence, governed by laws that defy our common-sense understanding of reality. The physical world, it turns out, is not as solid as it seems. It is a dynamic, ever-changing field of energy, where matter is merely a form that energy takes.

And yet, despite this deeper understanding of the physical world, we remain deeply tied to its surface appearance. We rely on our senses to tell us what is real, even though our senses are limited in their ability to perceive the full spectrum of reality. Our eyes can only see a tiny fraction of the electromagnetic spectrum, and our ears can only hear a limited range of frequencies. The physical dimension, as vast as it may seem, is but a thin slice of reality—a single layer in a multi-dimensional existence.

The Metaphysical Dimension: The Realm Beyond the Senses

Beyond the physical lies the metaphysical dimension—a realm that cannot be measured, weighed, or touched, yet it is as real as the physical world, if not more so. The word "metaphysical" comes from the Greek **meta** (beyond) and **physika** (nature), meaning that which is beyond the physical. It is the realm of mind, consciousness, spirit, and the deeper truths that underpin the universe.

The metaphysical dimension is often called the **invisible** or **non-material realm** because it does not conform to the same rules as the physical world. In this dimension, time is not linear, space is not bound by distance, and the limitations of the body no longer apply. Instead of relying on the senses, we access the metaphysical dimension through intuition, introspection, and heightened states of consciousness. This is the realm explored by mystics, philosophers, and spiritual seekers throughout history.

Imagine a moment of deep meditation, when the chatter of the mind fades, and a profound sense of stillness washes over you. In this stillness, the boundaries between the self and the world blur, and you experience a sense of interconnectedness with all that is. This is a glimpse into the metaphysical dimension. It is the space where the ego dissolves, where dualities such as "me" and "other," "here" and "there," cease to exist.

In the metaphysical realm, we encounter the deeper truths of existence—truths that cannot be fully grasped by the intellect alone. Concepts such as **unity, infinity, eternity**, and **oneness** emerge in this space. It is here that we realize the limitations of the physical dimension, recognizing that the world we see is but a projection of a deeper, underlying reality.

In many spiritual traditions, the metaphysical dimension is considered the **true** reality, while the physical world is seen as a temporary, illusory projection. This idea is central to the teachings of **Vedanta**, which describe the physical world as **Maya**, or illusion, while the metaphysical world is identified with **Brahman**, the infinite, eternal essence of all things. In this view, the physical world is not separate from the metaphysical; rather, it is an expression of the same underlying reality, filtered through the limited perception of the human mind.

The Intersection of the Physical and Metaphysical

While the physical and metaphysical dimensions may seem like two separate worlds, they are, in fact, deeply interconnected. The physical world is shaped by metaphysical forces, and the metaphysical world finds expression through the physical. Together, they form a continuous, layered reality, where the boundaries between the material and the non-material are fluid and ever-shifting.

Consider the relationship between thought and action. A thought—an intangible, metaphysical entity—can manifest in the physical world through action. For example, an architect envisions a building in their mind, and over time, that vision takes shape in the form of blueprints, construction, and, ultimately, a physical structure. In this way, the metaphysical realm of thought, intention, and imagination shapes the physical world.

The same can be said for the way emotions, which belong to the metaphysical realm, affect the body. Stress, a metaphysical state of mind, can lead to physical symptoms such as headaches, fatigue, and illness. Conversely, a sense of peace or joy can promote physical well-being. The mind-body connection is a clear example of how the metaphysical and physical dimensions are not separate but intertwined in ways that we are only beginning to understand.

Moreover, the metaphysical dimension provides the **meaning** and **purpose** that guide our actions in the physical world. Without the metaphysical dimension, the physical world would be devoid of deeper significance. Why do we strive for success, seek love, or create art? These pursuits are not driven by the physical necessities of survival alone. They are motivated by metaphysical desires for fulfillment, connection, and the realization of our highest potential.

The Seeker's Journey: Navigating the Layers of Reality

Throughout history, the greatest thinkers, mystics, and philosophers have sought to bridge the gap between the physical and metaphysical dimensions. They understood that to truly understand reality, one must look beyond the surface and explore the deeper layers of existence.

In the **Bhagavad Gita**, one of the foundational texts of Hindu philosophy, the hero Arjuna stands on the battlefield of life, torn between his duties in the physical world and his desire for spiritual understanding. His guide, Krishna, explains to him that true wisdom comes from recognizing the deeper, metaphysical truths that govern the universe. The battle, Krishna tells him, is not just a physical conflict but a reflection of the eternal struggle between ignorance and knowledge, between illusion and truth. Through this dialogue, Arjuna learns to navigate both the physical and metaphysical dimensions, realizing that his actions in the physical world are part of a larger, cosmic order.

Similarly, in **Buddhist philosophy**, the physical world is seen as a realm of **samsara**, or suffering, driven by attachment to impermanent forms. The path to enlightenment involves recognizing the illusory nature of the physical world and awakening to the deeper, metaphysical reality of **nirvana**, a state of pure being and liberation from the cycle of birth and death. For the seeker, this journey involves peeling away the layers of illusion, one by one, until only the truth remains.

In **Western philosophy**, thinkers such as **Plato** also grappled with the question of reality's layers. In his famous **Allegory of the Cave**, Plato describes a group of prisoners who are chained inside a cave, seeing only shadows on the wall, which they mistake for reality. It is only when one prisoner breaks free and ventures into the light of the outside world that he realizes the shadows were mere illusions, and that true reality lies beyond what the senses can perceive. For Plato, the physical world was like the cave—an imperfect reflection of the higher, metaphysical realm of **Forms**, where true knowledge and beauty reside.

These stories of seekers—Arjuna, the Buddha, Plato's prisoner—illustrate the timeless quest to understand the layers of reality. They remind us that while we live in the physical world, we are also part of something much greater, a vast metaphysical cosmos that holds the key to our deepest questions and longings.

The Role of Consciousness: The Bridge Between Worlds

At the heart of this exploration of the physical and metaphysical dimensions lies the mystery of **consciousness**. Consciousness is the bridge that connects the physical and metaphysical realms, allowing us to perceive, experience, and navigate both dimensions.

In the physical world, consciousness allows us to interact with the material environment, guiding our actions and decisions. But consciousness also opens the door to the metaphysical dimension, enabling us to reflect on our existence, contemplate deeper truths, and transcend the limitations of the physical body and mind.

Some philosophies suggest that consciousness itself is the ultimate reality, and that both the physical and metaphysical dimensions are expressions of this underlying consciousness. In **Advaita Vedanta**, for example, it is taught that the true self, or **Atman**, is not the body or the mind, but pure consciousness, which is identical to **Brahman**, the infinite and eternal reality. The physical world, in this view, is a manifestation of this consciousness, and by realizing our true nature, we can transcend the illusion of separation between the physical and metaphysical.

In modern science, the study of consciousness remains one of the most profound and elusive challenges. Despite advances in neuroscience, we have yet to fully understand how consciousness arises or how it interacts with the physical brain. Some scientists, like **David Chalmers**, have called this the "hard problem" of consciousness, suggesting that it may require us to rethink our understanding of reality itself. Could it be that consciousness is not just a product of the brain but a fundamental aspect of the universe, permeating both the physical and metaphysical dimensions?

Conclusion: Embracing the Mystery of Reality's Layers

As we stand at the intersection of the physical and metaphysical dimensions, we are faced with profound questions about the nature of reality and our place within it. The physical world, with all its beauty and complexity, is only the surface of a much deeper, more mysterious reality. Beneath this surface lies the metaphysical dimension, the realm of mind, spirit, and the infinite possibilities of existence.

The journey to understand these layers of reality is not just a philosophical or spiritual quest—it is a journey of self-discovery. It is a path that leads us to question what we know, to explore the unknown, and to embrace the mystery that lies at the heart of existence.

For the seeker, the layers of reality are not obstacles to be overcome but invitations to expand our understanding, to look beyond the limits of the physical world, and to explore the boundless realms of the metaphysical. And in doing so, we may come to realize that the physical and metaphysical are not two separate worlds but two sides of the same cosmic coin—a single, unified reality that is far more wondrous and vast than we can ever imagine.

- **Exploring the layers of consciousness**

In a world overflowing with distractions, the search for deeper understanding often leads us inward. Our minds are like vast landscapes, filled with intricate pathways and hidden chambers. Yet, how often do we truly explore the depths of our consciousness? This chapter invites you to embark on a journey—a journey that navigates the **layers of consciousness**, where we will uncover the various states of awareness that shape our perceptions, beliefs, and ultimately, our reality.

Imagine a seeker standing on the precipice of a great cliff, gazing into an expansive valley below. This valley represents the landscape of consciousness, filled with rivers of thought, mountains of emotion, and forests of memory. To truly explore this terrain, we must be willing to descend into its depths, examining the layers that form the foundation of our experience. Each layer is a vital part of the whole, revealing the multifaceted nature of consciousness itself.

The Surface Layer: Everyday Awareness

The first layer of consciousness we encounter is what we might call **everyday awareness**. This is the surface layer, the one we experience most frequently as we navigate our daily lives. It includes our thoughts, perceptions, and reactions to the external world. In this state, we are often preoccupied with the immediate demands of life: work, relationships, responsibilities, and the never-ending stream of information bombarding our senses.

In this everyday state of awareness, our minds are often cluttered. Thoughts flit by like autumn leaves caught in a gust of wind—some mundane, some significant, but all competing for our attention. We experience feelings and emotions that arise in response to our interactions with the world, and we react accordingly, often without conscious reflection. This is the layer of consciousness where we function, where we identify ourselves with our roles, our jobs, and our social identities.

Yet, within this seemingly ordinary layer lies a profound truth: everyday awareness is the gateway to deeper states of consciousness. It is a starting point, a foundation upon which we can build our understanding of the layers that lie beneath.

The Emotional Layer: The Heart's Resonance

As we venture deeper into the landscape of consciousness, we encounter the **emotional layer**. This layer is rich with feelings, sensations, and intuitions—an intricate tapestry woven from the threads of our experiences, traumas, joys, and sorrows. Here, we discover that emotions are not merely fleeting responses; they are essential elements that shape our perceptions and influence our actions.

Each emotion carries its own frequency, resonating through our being. Joy vibrates with a lightness that lifts us, while sadness can anchor us with its weight. Anger can burn fiercely, motivating us to act, while love can envelop us in warmth and connection. The emotional layer reveals the interconnectedness of our experiences, highlighting how our feelings are often responses to the external world, yet rooted in our inner landscape.

In this layer, we also encounter the concept of **emotional intelligence**—the ability to recognize, understand, and manage our emotions, as well as empathize with the emotions of others. Emotional intelligence allows us to navigate the complexities of relationships, to respond to situations with awareness rather than reaction. Through mindfulness practices, we can cultivate awareness of this emotional layer, gaining insight into how our feelings influence our perceptions and, ultimately, our consciousness.

The Subconscious Layer: The Repository of Memory

Beneath the emotional layer lies the **subconscious layer** of consciousness—a hidden reservoir of memories, beliefs, and patterns that shape our thoughts and behaviors. This layer is like an underground river, flowing beneath the surface and influencing our lives in subtle, often unnoticed ways.

The subconscious is home to our conditioning, the beliefs we adopted throughout our lives—beliefs about ourselves, about others, and about the world. Many of these beliefs were formed in childhood, shaped by our experiences, relationships, and the cultural context in which we were raised. They can become deeply embedded, influencing our actions and choices without our conscious awareness.

As the seeker descends further, they may encounter buried memories—traumas that have been locked away, experiences that have shaped their identity, and lessons that have been forgotten. These memories, whether positive or negative, continue to impact our lives, influencing our emotional responses and perceptions.

By exploring the subconscious layer, we can bring these hidden aspects into the light of awareness. Techniques such as journaling, dream analysis, and guided meditation can help illuminate the depths of our subconscious, allowing us to confront and heal past wounds. This process of excavation leads to greater self-awareness, enabling us to discern which beliefs serve us and which ones hold us back.

The Collective Unconscious: A Tapestry of Shared Experiences

Deeper still lies the **collective unconscious**, a concept introduced by the Swiss psychiatrist Carl Jung. This layer represents the shared reservoir of human experiences, archetypes, and symbols that transcend individual consciousness. Here, we tap into the wisdom of generations, accessing the collective knowledge, fears, and hopes that bind humanity together.

The collective unconscious is populated by archetypes—universal symbols and themes that recur across cultures and epochs. These include the Hero, the Mother, the Wise Old Man, and many others. These archetypes shape our narratives, influencing how we interpret our lives and the world around us. When we encounter a myth or a story that resonates deeply within us, we are tapping into this collective layer, drawing on the rich tapestry of human experience.

Exploring the collective unconscious invites us to consider our place in the grand narrative of humanity. It encourages us to recognize the interconnectedness of our individual journeys with the greater story of life.

Through art, literature, and spirituality, we can access this collective wisdom, finding guidance and inspiration in the shared experiences of others.

The Transcendent Layer: Unity and Oneness

As we reach the deepest layer of consciousness, we encounter the **transcendent layer**, often described as the realm of **unity**, **oneness**, and **pure awareness**. This layer transcends the individual self, revealing the interconnectedness of all existence. It is the layer where the seeker realizes that they are not separate from the universe, but an integral part of a greater whole.

In this transcendent state, distinctions between self and other dissolve. The boundaries of the ego fade away, revealing a sense of unity with all beings and the cosmos itself. This realization often comes through deep meditation, mystical experiences, or profound moments of insight.

Many spiritual traditions speak of this transcendent layer, describing it as the ultimate goal of human existence. In **Buddhism**, it is the realization of **nirvana**—the liberation from suffering and the cycle of rebirth. In **Hinduism**, it is the experience of **moksha**, the union of the individual soul with the divine source. In **Sufism**, it is the state of **fana**, where the self dissolves in the presence of the Divine.

As the seeker immerses themselves in this transcendent layer, they often report feelings of profound peace, love, and connection. Time becomes irrelevant; the past and future dissolve into the present moment. In this state of pure awareness, the seeker experiences the truth that beneath the layers of individual consciousness lies an infinite expanse of being—a reality where separation is an illusion, and unity is the essence of existence.

The Integration of Layers: A Holistic Approach to Consciousness

While we have explored the layers of consciousness as distinct realms, it is essential to recognize that they are interconnected and interdependent. Each layer influences the others, forming a complex web that shapes our experience of reality.

As the seeker ascends back to the surface, they carry with them the insights gained from each layer. The emotional layer informs their understanding of how feelings shape their thoughts; the subconscious layer reveals the beliefs that guide their actions; the collective unconscious provides a sense of belonging and purpose; and the transcendent layer offers a glimpse into the ultimate nature of existence.

To integrate these layers into a holistic understanding of consciousness, one must cultivate practices that honor each aspect of the self. Mindfulness, meditation, self-reflection, and expressive arts can serve as tools for navigating the landscape of consciousness, helping us to connect with our emotions, examine our beliefs, and access deeper states of awareness.

In this integration, the seeker learns to live in alignment with their true nature, recognizing the interplay between their inner world and the external reality. They become more adept at navigating challenges, making conscious choices, and embracing the complexities of existence with grace and compassion.

Conclusion: The Ongoing Journey of Consciousness

As we conclude our exploration of the layers of consciousness, we are reminded that this journey is not a destination but an ongoing process. The landscape of consciousness is vast, and there are always new depths to explore. Each layer offers a unique perspective, a new insight that enriches our understanding of ourselves and the world around us.

In a world filled with noise and distraction, the invitation remains: to venture inward, to explore the depths of our consciousness, and to awaken to the richness of our being. Through this exploration, we come to understand that we are not merely individuals navigating a separate existence but part of a grand tapestry of consciousness—woven together in a shared quest for meaning, connection, and truth.

The layers of consciousness are not just abstract concepts; they are the very essence of our humanity. By engaging with these layers, we can uncover the profound mysteries of existence, cultivating a deeper awareness of ourselves and our place in the cosmos. And in this journey of exploration, we may find that the true nature of consciousness is not just to perceive reality, but to co-create it—transforming our understanding of what it means to be alive.

- **The interplay of the material and spiritual worlds**

In the beginning, there was a great silence, a vast expanse of potential. From this silence emerged the first vibration, a subtle hum that reverberated through the void, weaving the fabric of existence. This primordial sound, known in many cultures as **Om**, is the essence of creation, the pulse of the universe that bridges the material and spiritual realms.

As we embark on this journey through the **interplay of the material and spiritual worlds**, we will explore how these two dimensions coexist, influence one another, and shape the human experience. This chapter invites you to witness the dance between the seen and the unseen, the tangible and the ethereal, as we uncover the profound truths that lie at the heart of existence.

The Material World: The Realm of Form

The material world is the domain of **form**—the tangible, visible universe where matter exists. It is where we encounter the physicality of life: the ground beneath our feet, the air we breathe, the bodies we inhabit. This world is governed by the laws of physics and biology, where atoms combine to form molecules, and molecules unite to create the vast diversity of life.

From the moment of birth, we are immersed in this material reality. We learn to navigate the physical environment through our senses, relying on sight, sound, touch, taste, and smell to interact with the world around us. The material world is rich with textures and colors, experiences that ignite our emotions, and relationships that shape our identity.

Yet, for all its beauty and complexity, the material world can also feel limiting. Our experiences are often bound by time and space, and we may find ourselves caught in the cycle of desire and attachment. We strive for success, acquire possessions, and seek validation from the external world, believing that happiness lies in the material.

However, this quest for fulfillment in the material realm often leads to a sense of emptiness. We may find that despite our achievements, we still yearn for something more—a deeper connection, a greater purpose, a sense of belonging to something beyond the physical.

The Spiritual World: The Realm of Essence

As we venture into the **spiritual world**, we enter a realm that transcends the limitations of the material. The spiritual dimension is where we encounter the **essence** of existence—an infinite, boundless expanse that is often described as pure consciousness, love, or divine energy. It is the realm of the unseen, where thoughts, emotions, and intentions hold power beyond the physical manifestation.

In the spiritual world, we begin to uncover our true nature. Here, we are not defined by our possessions, achievements, or roles but by the light that resides within us. The spiritual realm invites us to explore questions of meaning, purpose, and interconnectedness. It urges us to look beyond the superficial aspects of life and delve into the depths of our being.

Through practices such as meditation, prayer, and introspection, we can access the spiritual dimension. In moments of stillness, we may experience a sense of unity with all that exists—a realization that we are interconnected threads woven into the grand tapestry of life. This sense of connection transcends individual identity, revealing a greater truth: that we are all expressions of the same divine essence.

Yet, while the spiritual world offers profound insights and experiences, it is not separate from the material. Rather, it exists in a dynamic interplay with the physical realm, shaping and influencing our experiences in ways that are often subtle and profound.

The Dance Between Worlds

The interplay between the material and spiritual worlds can be likened to a dance—a delicate choreography where each realm informs and enhances the other. Just as the physical body serves as a vessel for the spirit, the spiritual dimension offers guidance and meaning to our material existence.

Consider the story of a talented musician, whose melodies evoke emotions that resonate deeply within the hearts of listeners. In their practice, the musician must master the physicality of their instrument, learning to navigate the complexities of technique and rhythm. Yet, it is in moments of inspiration—when they feel a deep connection to something greater—that the music transcends mere notes and becomes a profound expression of the spiritual.

In these moments, the musician taps into the spiritual realm, channeling emotions, experiences, and intentions into their art. The resulting composition becomes a bridge between the material and spiritual worlds, allowing others to connect with the deeper truths of existence.

This interplay can also be observed in the natural world. The changing seasons, the cycle of life and death, and the beauty of a sunrise all reflect the dynamic relationship between the material and spiritual. Nature serves as a reminder that the physical world is imbued with spiritual significance, inviting us to pause, reflect, and appreciate the interconnectedness of all life.

The Influence of Intentions and Energy

At the heart of the interplay between the material and spiritual worlds lies the concept of **intention** and **energy**. Our thoughts and beliefs shape our experiences, influencing how we perceive reality. When we cultivate positive intentions, we raise our energetic vibration, creating a ripple effect that extends into the material realm.

The practice of **manifestation**, popularized in modern spirituality, illustrates this connection. It emphasizes the power of thoughts and intentions in shaping our reality. By focusing on what we desire—be it love, abundance, or healing—we align our energy with the frequencies of those experiences. This alignment allows us to attract corresponding opportunities and circumstances in the material world.

Consider the story of a woman named Maya, who had long dreamt of starting her own business. After years of working in a corporate job that left her unfulfilled, she began to explore the spiritual dimensions of her desires. Through meditation and visualization, Maya clarified her intentions, envisioning not only her business but also the impact she wanted to have on her community.

As she aligned her energy with her vision, opportunities began to manifest. She met like-minded individuals who shared her passion, and soon, her dream became a reality. Maya's journey illustrates how the interplay of intention and energy can shape our experiences in the material world, bridging the gap between the spiritual and physical dimensions.

The Role of Challenges and Growth

The interplay between the material and spiritual worlds is not always smooth; it can be fraught with challenges and obstacles. Life's difficulties—loss, grief, disappointment—serve as catalysts for spiritual growth. These experiences often push us to confront our beliefs, reevaluate our priorities, and seek deeper meaning in our lives.

Consider the story of a man named Ravi, who faced a devastating loss when his wife passed away unexpectedly. In the aftermath of his grief, he found himself questioning the very fabric of reality. As he navigated his sorrow, Ravi sought solace in spirituality. He began attending meditation retreats, engaging in deep introspection, and exploring the teachings of various spiritual traditions.

Through this journey, Ravi discovered that his pain was not separate from his spiritual growth. His loss compelled him to confront his beliefs about love, life, and death. As he processed his grief, he unearthed profound insights about the nature of existence and the interconnectedness of all beings.

Ravi learned that the challenges of the material world often serve as gateways to spiritual awakening. In this way, the interplay between the two realms fosters growth, resilience, and transformation. By embracing life's difficulties, we open ourselves to deeper understanding and connection.

The Path of Integration

As we navigate the interplay of the material and spiritual worlds, we are invited to cultivate a path of integration—a harmonious blending of both dimensions. This journey encourages us to honor the material aspects of life while simultaneously deepening our connection to the spiritual.

Integration begins with awareness. By recognizing the influence of the material world on our spiritual beliefs and vice versa, we can cultivate a more holistic understanding of our experiences. We learn to appreciate the beauty of life's joys while also acknowledging the lessons embedded within challenges.

Practices such as **mindfulness**, **gratitude**, and **compassion** serve as bridges between the two realms. Mindfulness allows us to fully engage with the present moment, whether we are savoring a meal, enjoying a conversation, or experiencing a moment of stillness. Gratitude invites us to acknowledge the abundance in our lives, shifting our focus from lack to appreciation. Compassion opens our hearts to the struggles of others, fostering connection and empathy.

The journey of integration also involves recognizing the sacredness of the ordinary. The material world, often perceived as mundane, holds profound spiritual significance. Every experience, whether joyful or challenging, is an opportunity for growth and exploration. By approaching life with a sense of wonder and reverence, we can uncover the spiritual essence woven into the fabric of everyday existence.

Conclusion: Embracing the Interplay

As we conclude our exploration of the interplay between the material and spiritual worlds, we are reminded that these realms are not opposing forces but complementary aspects of our existence. Each layer enriches our understanding of reality, guiding us toward deeper awareness, connection, and purpose.

In this intricate dance, we discover that we are not mere observers of the material world but active participants in the unfolding of the spiritual. Our thoughts, intentions, and actions shape our experiences, allowing us to co-create our reality with the universe.

By embracing the interplay of the material and spiritual, we awaken to the truth that life is a sacred journey—a tapestry woven from the threads of our experiences, emotions, and aspirations. As we navigate this journey, we invite ourselves to be fully present, to engage with the richness of existence, and to honor the divine essence that flows through all things.

In this way, the interplay of the material and spiritual worlds becomes a source of inspiration and guidance, inviting us to explore the depths of our being and to celebrate the beauty of our shared humanity. Through this exploration, we may find that the true essence of life lies not in the separation of these worlds, but in their harmonious union—a dance that reflects the infinite possibilities of existence.

Chapter 4: The Role of Divine Play (Lila)

- **Understanding Lila in the context of Yogamaya**

In the grand theater of existence, where the material and spiritual intertwine, there lies a concept as profound as it is playful: **Lila**, or the Divine Play. It is the very essence of creation, a cosmic dance that unfolds within the heart of **Yogamaya**, the divine illusion that shapes our perceptions and experiences. To understand Lila is to glimpse the underlying rhythm of the universe, where the sacred and the mundane harmonize in a timeless ballet.

Imagine the universe as a vast stage, where actors and actresses—embodied souls—perform their roles in a grand drama orchestrated by the Divine. Each soul, unique in its essence, carries within it the spark of the divine, the breath of creation that infuses life with purpose and meaning. Yet, the nature of this performance is multifaceted, encompassing joy and sorrow, love and loss, success and failure. It is in the context of Lila that we find the truth of existence: that life is a play, and we are both the actors and the spectators.

The Essence of Lila

To comprehend Lila, we must first explore its roots in **Yogamaya**—the divine energy that creates the illusion of separation and multiplicity. In this cosmic play, Yogamaya acts as the veil that obscures the ultimate reality, allowing us to experience life in its myriad forms. It is the creative force that brings forth the diversity of existence, giving rise to the myriad expressions of consciousness.

Yogamaya creates a world where the divine can interact with itself through the medium of form. It is the matrix that allows the infinite to become finite, the eternal to experience the temporal. Within this context, Lila emerges as the playful manifestation of the Divine's creative impulse.

The term Lila is often translated as "play" or "sport," but it carries deeper connotations. It suggests a sense of spontaneity, joy, and freedom—a divine expression that is both intentional and playful. The divine engages in this cosmic dance, creating and dissolving worlds, manifesting and withdrawing, all while inviting us to participate in this unfolding drama.

The Divine Play of Creation

Consider the story of **Krishna**, the embodiment of Lila in Hindu tradition. From his childhood antics of stealing butter to his enchanting dance with the gopis (cowherd girls) of Vrindavan, Krishna's life is a tapestry of playful divine expressions. Each of his exploits illustrates the nature of Lila—a reminder that life is not a solemn affair but a joyful celebration of existence.

In one tale, Krishna plays the flute, its enchanting melodies drawing the gopis to him. As they dance together in the moonlight, they are enveloped in the bliss of divine love, transcending their worldly concerns. This dance represents the ecstatic union of the individual soul (jiva) with the Supreme Consciousness (Brahman), illustrating the transformative power of divine love and play.

In this context, Lila is not merely an abstract concept but a lived experience. It invites us to participate in the cosmic dance, to embrace the joy and spontaneity of life. Each moment becomes an opportunity for expression, a chance to engage with the divine within and around us.

The Illusion of Separation

Yet, the interplay of Lila and Yogamaya also brings forth the illusion of separation. While the divine play unfolds, we often find ourselves lost in the narratives of our individual lives, believing in the reality of our separateness. This is the nature of Yogamaya—it obscures the truth of our interconnectedness and the unity of existence.

In the material world, we may identify with our roles, our desires, and our fears, forgetting that these are but fleeting aspects of the play. We become attached to our experiences, leading to suffering when they do not unfold as we wish. In this state of identification, we lose sight of the divine purpose behind Lila, becoming entangled in the web of desires and attachments.

However, the beauty of Lila lies in its ability to guide us back to the truth. Through the dance of life, we are invited to transcend our limited perspectives and reconnect with the divine essence that resides within us.

Awakening Through Lila

The path of awakening through Lila involves recognizing that life is a play—a play that invites us to engage fully, yet not to be ensnared by its illusions. As we embrace the role of the actor in this cosmic drama, we begin to cultivate a sense of detachment—a realization that while our experiences are real, they are also transient.

Through practices such as **yoga**, **meditation**, and **devotional worship**, we learn to witness the play of life from a place of awareness. In this space, we can observe our thoughts and emotions without becoming overwhelmed by them. We begin to see the patterns of our desires and fears, understanding that they are part of the grand design of Lila.

In this awakening, we rediscover the joy of being alive—the spontaneity and wonder that often eludes us in the rush of daily life. We learn to celebrate the small moments: a shared laugh with a friend, the beauty of nature, the joy of creativity. Each experience becomes a reminder of the divine play, an invitation to engage fully with life while remaining anchored in the awareness of our true nature.

The Role of Suffering in Lila

One of the paradoxes of Lila is the presence of suffering within the divine play. Just as joy and laughter are integral to the cosmic dance, so too are pain and sorrow. The interplay of these emotions serves as a reminder of the impermanence of existence—a vital aspect of the human experience.

Consider the story of **Rama**, another incarnation of the divine, who faced immense trials and tribulations throughout his life. From his exile in the forest to the abduction of his beloved Sita, Rama's journey is marked by suffering. Yet, each challenge becomes an opportunity for growth and transformation, leading him closer to his ultimate purpose.

In this light, suffering is not to be feared or avoided; it is an integral part of Lila. It teaches us resilience, compassion, and empathy. Through our struggles, we learn to appreciate joy more deeply, to understand the interconnectedness of all beings, and to cultivate love and kindness in the face of adversity.

The acknowledgment of suffering within the divine play also invites us to extend compassion to ourselves and others. When we recognize that we are all navigating the complexities of existence, we can approach one another with grace and understanding. We begin to see the divine spark in every individual, regardless of their circumstances, and we are moved to engage in acts of love and service.

Embracing the Play

As we deepen our understanding of Lila in the context of Yogamaya, we are invited to embrace the divine play as a vital aspect of our journey. Life is not a burden to be endured but a dance to be celebrated. By recognizing the interplay between the material and spiritual realms, we can cultivate a sense of joy and spontaneity that infuses every moment.

In practical terms, embracing Lila means allowing ourselves to experience life fully without clinging to outcomes. It means recognizing that while we may strive for certain goals, the journey itself is where the richness lies. It invites us to approach challenges with a sense of curiosity, to see them as opportunities for growth rather than obstacles.

This approach also encourages us to cultivate a sense of humor—a lightness of being that allows us to navigate the ups and downs of life with grace. In the face of adversity, we can learn to laugh at the absurdities of existence, to find joy even in the darkest moments.

Conclusion: The Divine Invitation

In conclusion, the role of Divine Play (Lila) within the context of Yogamaya offers us profound insights into the nature of existence. It invites us to recognize the interplay between the material and spiritual realms, to celebrate the dance of life, and to embrace the joy and spontaneity that come from engaging fully in the cosmic drama.

As we navigate our journeys, may we remember that we are not mere spectators but active participants in the divine play. Each moment is an invitation to dance, to express ourselves, and to connect with the essence of life that flows through all beings.

Through Lila, we find the courage to embrace the entirety of our experiences—the joy, the sorrow, the triumphs, and the challenges. We learn to see life as a sacred journey, where every step is infused with meaning and purpose. And in this recognition, we discover the profound truth that beneath the surface of existence lies the divine spark that connects us all—a reminder that we are, at our core, expressions of the same cosmic dance.

- **The purpose of divine play in the universe**

In the vast expanse of the cosmos, where galaxies spin and stars twinkle in the velvet night, there lies an intricate dance—a **Divine Play** that unfolds with a purpose as profound as the universe itself. This play, known as **Lila**, is not merely a whimsical performance but a sacred expression of the cosmos, a symphony of existence that invites every soul to participate in the unfolding of reality.

To understand the purpose of this divine play, we must embark on a journey—a journey that weaves together the threads of creation, consciousness, and connection. As we delve into this exploration, we will discover that the purpose of Lila is not only to entertain or amuse, but to illuminate the path of existence, guide spiritual evolution, and reveal the profound truth of our interconnectedness.

The Nature of Creation

At the heart of the Divine Play lies the essence of **creation**. The universe is not a static entity but a living, breathing manifestation of divine consciousness. From the first flicker of light that split the darkness to the formation of stars and planets, every aspect of creation embodies the playful nature of the Divine.

This cosmic creativity invites us to witness the beauty and complexity of life. Consider the story of **Brahma**, the creator in Hindu mythology, who is often depicted as engaging in a divine play as he shapes the world. With each thought, each intention, he brings forth new forms of life—mountains, rivers, animals, and humans—each a reflection of the divine essence that flows through all things.

Through this creative process, Lila reveals that existence is a celebration—a joyful expression of diversity and multiplicity. The myriad forms of life, from the smallest microbe to the largest galaxy, are threads in the grand tapestry of the universe. Each thread plays a unique role, contributing to the overall harmony of creation.

The Journey of Self-Discovery

Within the Divine Play, the purpose of existence extends beyond mere survival; it is a journey of **self-discovery**. Each soul incarnated in the physical realm embarks on a unique path, guided by the playful hand of the Divine. Through experiences of joy, suffering, love, and loss, we are invited to explore the depths of our being and uncover the truths that lie within.

As we navigate the complexities of life, we are encouraged to ask questions: Who am I? What is my purpose? How do I connect with others and the world around me? The challenges and triumphs we encounter serve as mirrors, reflecting the deeper aspects of our consciousness.

Consider the story of **Sita**, the beloved wife of Rama, who faced immense trials during her journey in the Ramayana. Captured by the demon king Ravana, Sita's strength and resilience were tested to their limits. Yet, within the depths of her suffering, she discovered her inner power and unwavering devotion.

Sita's journey illustrates how the Divine Play serves as a catalyst for self-realization. Through the lens of Lila, we learn that challenges are not obstacles but opportunities for growth. Each experience offers insights into our true nature, guiding us toward the realization that we are expressions of the divine, interconnected with all of creation.

The Dance of Interconnectedness

One of the most profound purposes of Divine Play is to reveal the **interconnectedness** of all beings. In the vast cosmic dance, every soul is a note in the symphony of existence. The laughter of a child, the rustle of leaves, the song of a bird—all resonate with the vibrations of life, echoing the fundamental truth that we are never truly alone.

In this dance, Lila teaches us the importance of relationships. Our connections with others, whether through love, friendship, or compassion, reflect the divine nature of creation. As we engage in this play, we learn to see the divine in every face, to recognize that each interaction is an opportunity for connection and growth.

Imagine a great river, flowing through mountains and valleys, connecting disparate landscapes. Each tributary that joins the river represents an individual soul, contributing to the larger flow of existence. Just as the river nourishes the land, our relationships nourish our spirits, allowing us to grow and flourish.

This interconnectedness invites us to cultivate empathy and compassion. When we recognize that every being is part of the divine play, we are compelled to treat others with kindness and respect. We learn that our actions ripple through the fabric of existence, impacting not only our lives but the lives of countless others.

The Catalyst for Spiritual Evolution

At its core, the Divine Play serves as a **catalyst for spiritual evolution**. The experiences we encounter, the lessons we learn, and the relationships we forge all contribute to our growth as spiritual beings. As we engage in the dance of Lila, we are invited to evolve, to expand our consciousness, and to deepen our understanding of the universe.

The concept of **Karma** plays a significant role in this evolution. Each action we take sends forth vibrations that resonate throughout the cosmos, shaping our future experiences. In this sense, Lila becomes a playground of opportunities—where every choice, thought, and intention contributes to our spiritual journey.

Consider the tale of **Arjuna** from the Mahabharata, who stood on the battlefield faced with a moral dilemma. Torn between duty and compassion, Arjuna's journey toward self-realization exemplifies the transformative power of Lila. Guided by Krishna, he learns to navigate the complexities of life with wisdom and discernment, ultimately awakening to his higher purpose.

Through Arjuna's journey, we see that the Divine Play challenges us to confront our limitations, question our beliefs, and transcend the confines of our ego. It encourages us to embrace our inherent divinity and recognize our role as co-creators of reality.

The Celebration of Existence

Another essential purpose of Divine Play is to invite us to celebrate existence itself. Life, with all its ups and downs, is a gift—a precious opportunity to experience the richness of the universe. In the grand tapestry of Lila, every moment becomes a chance to appreciate the beauty, wonder, and mystery of creation.

The act of celebration is woven into the fabric of many spiritual traditions. Festivals, rituals, and gatherings serve as expressions of gratitude for the divine gifts bestowed upon us. They remind us to pause and appreciate the miracles that unfold in our lives, whether they are grand or seemingly mundane.

Consider the vibrant festivals of **Holi** and **Diwali**, celebrated in India. Holi, the festival of colors, symbolizes the arrival of spring and the victory of good over evil. Participants joyfully throw colored powders, dance, and sing, celebrating the vibrancy of life. Similarly, Diwali, the festival of lights, represents the triumph of light over darkness, inviting us to illuminate our inner selves.

Through these celebrations, we are reminded that life is not merely a series of struggles but a joyous dance of existence. We learn to embrace the present moment, to find joy in the simple pleasures, and to express gratitude for the beauty that surrounds us.

The Invitation to Play

As we reflect on the purpose of Divine Play in the universe, we are invited to embrace the spirit of playfulness in our own lives. The journey of existence is not meant to be taken too seriously; rather, it invites us to engage with life as an adventure—a canvas for creativity, exploration, and growth.

To embody this spirit, we must cultivate curiosity—the willingness to approach each day with an open heart and mind. This involves letting go of preconceived notions and allowing ourselves to explore the unknown. Whether it's trying a new hobby, engaging in meaningful conversations, or exploring the beauty of nature, every experience becomes an opportunity for discovery.

Moreover, we are invited to release the burdens of perfectionism and control. In the Divine Play, there is no need to have all the answers or to execute every action flawlessly. Instead, we are encouraged to embrace our imperfections and learn from our mistakes. This lightness allows us to engage with life more fully, freeing us to experience the richness of the moment.

Conclusion: The Eternal Dance

In conclusion, the purpose of Divine Play in the universe is a multifaceted expression of existence—a celebration of creation, a journey of self-discovery, an exploration of interconnectedness, a catalyst for spiritual evolution, and an invitation to celebrate life. As we navigate this cosmic dance, we are reminded that we are both participants and witnesses to the grand tapestry of Lila.

Through our experiences, we learn that life is not a linear path but a dynamic interplay of joys and sorrows, triumphs and challenges. Each moment, each interaction, and each choice contributes to the unfolding of our spiritual journey.

As we embrace the spirit of playfulness, we awaken to the beauty and wonder of existence. We discover that life is a sacred gift—an opportunity to express our unique essence and connect with the divine. In this realization, we find the courage to dance, to laugh, to love, and to engage with the world around us.

In the eternal dance of Divine Play, we come to understand that we are not separate from the universe; we are an integral part of it. As we celebrate the interplay of existence, we awaken to the truth that life is, at its core, a divine expression—a reflection of the infinite possibilities that reside within each of us.

- **How Lila creates the illusion of separateness**

In the intricate fabric of existence, the concept of **Lila** serves as a profound force that shapes our experience of reality. As the Divine Play of the universe, Lila embodies both creativity and illusion, weaving a tapestry that reflects the complexity of life. At its core, Lila creates the illusion of **separateness**, enabling each soul to experience individuality and uniqueness in a world that is, in essence, interconnected and whole.

To comprehend how Lila manifests this illusion, we must embark on a journey through the realms of creation, perception, and consciousness. As we traverse this landscape, we will uncover the purpose behind the illusion of separateness and its role in our spiritual evolution.

The Nature of Reality

To understand the illusion of separateness, we must first explore the nature of reality itself. In the vast cosmos, every particle, every thought, and every emotion is intricately interconnected. The ancient wisdom of many spiritual traditions teaches us that beneath the surface of diversity lies a profound unity—a singular consciousness that permeates all existence.

This unity can be likened to the ocean and its waves. The ocean represents the ultimate reality, while the waves symbolize the individual expressions of that reality. Each wave is unique in its form, size, and movement, yet it is never separate from the ocean from which it arises. It is in this metaphor that we begin to see how Lila operates.

In the grand play of Lila, the Divine orchestrates the emergence of myriad forms and experiences, allowing each wave to rise and fall, to dance and frolic on the surface of the ocean. However, in doing so, the waves often forget their origin, perceiving themselves as distinct entities rather than expressions of the same vast ocean.

The Veil of Yogamaya

Integral to the experience of separateness is the concept of **Yogamaya**, the divine energy that creates the veil of illusion. Yogamaya allows the infinite to manifest as finite forms, obscuring the underlying unity of existence. It acts as a filter through which we perceive reality, shaping our experiences and guiding our perceptions.

Imagine walking through a lush forest, where sunlight filters through the leaves, casting dappled shadows on the ground. The beauty of the forest enchants the senses, drawing one's attention to the individual trees, flowers, and animals. Yet, the experience can lead one to forget that all these elements are interconnected, part of the same ecosystem, thriving together in harmony.

Yogamaya allows us to experience the richness of life in all its diversity, but it can also create a sense of separation—a belief that we are distinct from the world around us. This veil is necessary for our journey; it enables us to explore the depths of our individuality, to forge our identities, and to learn valuable lessons along the way.

The Role of Individual Experience

The illusion of separateness plays a crucial role in the journey of self-discovery. Each soul is born into a unique set of circumstances, carrying its own history, emotions, and experiences. This individual narrative is essential for growth, as it allows us to explore the many facets of existence.

Consider the story of **Ravi**, a young man born into a family of artists. From a young age, Ravi was encouraged to express himself through painting, dance, and music. As he grew, he developed a distinct style that reflected his inner world—a vivid expression of his individuality.

However, as Ravi pursued his artistic passion, he became increasingly aware of the pressure to conform to societal expectations. The more he sought external validation, the more he felt separated from his true self. This experience of separateness fueled a deep internal struggle, leading Ravi on a quest for authenticity.

Through his journey, Ravi came to understand that the illusion of separateness serves a purpose. It allows us to explore our unique gifts and talents, to encounter challenges that lead to growth, and to forge connections with others who resonate with our experiences. Each individual story contributes to the larger narrative of existence, enriching the divine play of Lila.

The Dance of Duality

The experience of separateness is further magnified by the interplay of **duality**—the contrast between light and dark, joy and sorrow, love and fear. This duality is an essential aspect of life, allowing us to appreciate the fullness of existence. Just as night gives way to day, our experiences of pleasure and pain provide the backdrop for our personal growth.

The dualistic nature of reality creates a sense of distinction between the self and the other. In relationships, we may perceive ourselves as separate from those we love or those we struggle to understand. This perception can lead to misunderstandings and conflicts, but it also offers opportunities for deeper connection and empathy.

For example, consider the story of **Meera**, a woman deeply in love with the divine. As she devoted herself to her spiritual practice, she found herself longing for union with the divine essence. However, her yearning was often clouded by feelings of separation, as if the divine was distant and unattainable.

Through her struggles, Meera began to see that the very separation she felt was a part of the divine play—a dance between her individual self and the higher self. It was through her longing and devotion that she would ultimately come to realize that she was never truly separate from the divine. The illusion of separateness became a catalyst for her spiritual awakening.

The Path of Surrender

As we navigate the illusion of separateness, we are invited to embrace the path of **surrender**. Surrendering to the divine play means recognizing that while we may experience ourselves as separate individuals, we are also part of a greater whole. It involves letting go of the need to control our circumstances and allowing life to unfold in its own rhythm.

This surrender does not imply passivity; rather, it encourages active engagement with life. It invites us to cultivate trust in the process of existence, to understand that each experience serves a purpose in our spiritual evolution. The more we surrender to the flow of life, the more we can appreciate the interconnectedness of all beings.

In the story of **Sadhana**, a wise woman who lived in a small village, we find a profound example of surrender. Sadhana had experienced many hardships throughout her life—loss, illness, and disappointment. Yet, she approached each challenge with grace and acceptance. Rather than resisting the currents of life, she surrendered to them, trusting that they would lead her to greater wisdom.

As Sadhana continued her journey, she began to notice the threads that connected her to others. The villagers would seek her guidance, drawn to her radiant presence. In her surrender, Sadhana discovered that the illusion of separateness was merely a veil obscuring the profound unity she shared with her community.

The Awakening to Unity

Through the lens of Lila, the ultimate purpose of the illusion of separateness is to facilitate our awakening to unity. The divine play encourages us to navigate our individual journeys while gradually recognizing that we are all part of the same cosmic dance.

As we peel back the layers of illusion, we begin to see the interconnected web of existence. The pain we inflict on others reflects our own suffering; the love we share is a glimpse of the divine essence within us. This awakening to unity invites us to cultivate compassion, empathy, and understanding in our relationships.

Consider the tale of **Anaya**, a young woman who had long felt isolated in her struggles. She carried the weight of her challenges in silence, believing that no one could truly understand her pain. However, through a series of serendipitous encounters, she began to connect with others who shared similar experiences.

In these connections, Anaya discovered the truth of her existence: that her struggles were not unique but part of the collective human experience. As she opened her heart to others, she found healing, understanding, and a sense of belonging. The illusion of separateness began to dissolve, revealing the profound unity that existed beneath the surface.

Embracing the Play

As we navigate the complexities of Lila and the illusion of separateness, we are invited to embrace the play of life with open arms. This embrace involves recognizing that our individual experiences, while unique, are woven into the larger tapestry of existence.

Each encounter, each challenge, and each moment of joy becomes an integral part of the divine play, enriching our journey and the journeys of those around us. By embracing this perspective, we cultivate a sense of gratitude for the myriad experiences life offers.

In practical terms, this means approaching each day as a new opportunity for exploration and connection. Whether it's engaging in meaningful conversations, immersing ourselves in nature, or expressing creativity, every moment becomes a chance to celebrate the divine play unfolding within and around us.

Conclusion: The Illusion as a Gift

In conclusion, the illusion of separateness created by Lila serves a vital purpose in our spiritual evolution. It allows us to explore our individuality, engage in the dance of duality, and ultimately awaken to the unity that underlies all existence.

Through our journeys, we learn that separateness is not a curse but a gift—a sacred opportunity to engage with the divine play of life. As we navigate the intricate tapestry of existence, may we remember that while we may appear as distinct threads, we are all part of the same cosmic fabric.

In the grand design of Lila, the illusion of separateness invites us to cultivate love, compassion, and understanding. It encourages us to embrace the richness of our individual stories while recognizing that we are, at our core, expressions of the same divine essence.

As we dance through the sacred play of life, may we awaken to the profound truth that we are never truly separate, but always connected in the eternal embrace of the cosmos.

Chapter 5: Awakening from the Illusion

- Signs of spiritual awakening

In the quiet corners of existence, a subtle yet profound transformation begins to unfold within the hearts of seekers. This transformation, known as **spiritual awakening**, marks the dawning of a new consciousness—a journey that transcends the confines of the mundane and leads one toward the realization of their true essence. As the veil of illusion lifts, individuals begin to perceive the world through a lens of clarity, compassion, and connection.

But what are the signs of this spiritual awakening? How does one recognize that they are being called to embark on this sacred journey? To understand this profound phenomenon, we must explore the myriad experiences and shifts in perception that accompany awakening, weaving together a narrative that illuminates the path of transformation.

The Discontent of the Soul

Often, the journey of awakening begins with a deep sense of **discontent**—a feeling that something is amiss in one's life. This discontent can manifest as a pervasive sense of emptiness, a longing for deeper meaning, or a recognition that the conventional pursuits of happiness are ultimately unfulfilling. It is as if a quiet voice within whispers, "There must be more to life than this."

Consider the story of **Anika**, a successful corporate executive who appeared to have it all: a prestigious job, a beautiful home, and a busy social life. Yet, beneath the polished surface, Anika felt a gnawing emptiness that she could not ignore. Despite her achievements, she sensed that she was living a life dictated by societal expectations rather than her true desires.

This discontent serves as a catalyst for spiritual awakening. It is the soul's way of urging us to look beyond the surface and question the deeper aspects of our existence. As Anika began to explore her inner world, she realized that her true passion lay in helping others, a realization that set her on a path toward authenticity.

Heightened Awareness and Perception

As the awakening process unfolds, individuals often experience a **heightened awareness** of their thoughts, emotions, and surroundings. This expanded consciousness allows them to perceive the interconnectedness of all things, fostering a sense of unity with the universe. Suddenly, the mundane becomes extraordinary; the beauty of a sunset, the laughter of a child, or the rustle of leaves resonates deeply within.

Imagine **Ravi**, a once-disillusioned artist who spent years lost in the noise of the city. One evening, as he wandered through a park, he felt an inexplicable urge to pause and absorb the world around him. The vibrant colors of the flowers, the symphony of birdsong, and the gentle caress of the breeze enveloped him in a profound sense of peace. In that moment, Ravi recognized the beauty that had always existed but had gone unnoticed amidst the chaos of life.

This heightened awareness often leads to a deep sense of gratitude for the present moment. Individuals may find themselves marveling at the intricacies of life, realizing that every experience—whether joyous or painful—contributes to their journey of growth and understanding.

Emotional Release and Healing

As the layers of illusion dissolve, individuals may also encounter a profound **emotional release**. Old wounds, traumas, and unresolved issues rise to the surface, demanding acknowledgment and healing. This process can be challenging; it often involves confronting suppressed emotions, fears, and insecurities that have been buried for far too long.

Take the journey of **Maya**, a young woman who had experienced deep loss in her life. After years of repression, she found herself overwhelmed by memories that resurfaced during her meditation practice. Instead of shying away from the pain, Maya embraced it, allowing herself to grieve fully. Through tears and vulnerability, she discovered a strength within her that she never knew existed.

This emotional release is a vital sign of spiritual awakening. It signals a willingness to confront the shadows of the past, to heal and transform, and to embrace authenticity. As individuals honor their emotions, they pave the way for deeper self-acceptance and growth.

Intuition and Inner Guidance

With spiritual awakening often comes an enhanced sense of **intuition**. Individuals begin to trust their inner voice and instincts, feeling more aligned with their true selves. This intuitive knowing often guides them toward decisions that resonate with their authentic purpose, helping them navigate life's complexities with grace and clarity.

Consider **Arjun**, a businessman who had spent years chasing financial success at the expense of his well-being. After a series of transformative experiences, he began to listen to his intuition more closely. Instead of relying solely on logic, Arjun learned to tune into his feelings and instincts when making choices.

One day, he felt an overwhelming urge to volunteer at a local shelter. Despite his initial hesitation, he followed that intuitive nudge. This decision not only brought him joy but also connected him with a community that resonated with his values. Through this experience, Arjun recognized that his true purpose extended beyond financial gain; it involved serving others and making a positive impact in the world.

A Shift in Values and Priorities

As individuals awaken, they often experience a **shift in values** and priorities. Material possessions, status, and societal approval lose their allure, making way for a deeper appreciation of experiences, relationships, and personal growth. This shift prompts individuals to reassess their lives and align their actions with their evolving values.

Imagine **Leila**, a young professional who spent years climbing the corporate ladder, believing that success was synonymous with happiness. As she awakened to her true self, she realized that her greatest joy came from meaningful connections with friends and family. Determined to prioritize her relationships, Leila made the bold decision to step back from her demanding job and create a more balanced life.

This shift in values can lead to profound transformations, as individuals embrace their true passions and redefine their sense of fulfillment. They become more attuned to the needs of their hearts, seeking out experiences that nurture their souls and enrich their lives.

Compassion and Empathy

One of the most beautiful signs of spiritual awakening is the emergence of **compassion and empathy**. As individuals recognize their interconnectedness with all beings, their hearts open to the struggles and joys of others. This newfound awareness fosters a deep sense of compassion, prompting individuals to extend kindness and understanding to those around them.

Consider the journey of **Nisha**, a nurse who dedicated her life to caring for others. As Nisha awakened to her spiritual path, she discovered a profound sense of empathy that transcended her professional role. She began to see her patients not just as individuals seeking medical care but as fellow souls on their own journeys.

Nisha's compassion deepened as she listened to their stories and connected with their emotions. This connection not only enhanced her ability to heal but also illuminated the shared humanity that bound them all together. Through her awakening, Nisha learned that compassion is a powerful force that can transform lives, including her own.

Synchronicities and Signs

As individuals progress on their spiritual journeys, they often encounter **synchronicities**—meaningful coincidences that seem to guide them along their path. These signs from the universe can manifest in various forms, such as repeating numbers, chance encounters, or serendipitous events that align with their intentions.

Take the story of **Vikram**, a man who had recently begun to explore spirituality. One evening, while walking home, he stumbled upon a bookshop that caught his eye. Inside, he discovered a book that spoke directly to his current struggles and aspirations. The author's words resonated deeply within him, providing clarity and guidance.

Moments like these are not mere coincidences; they are messages from the universe, affirming that individuals are on the right path. As people open their hearts and minds to the possibility of synchronicity, they become more attuned to the guidance that surrounds them.

A Deepening Connection to Nature

With spiritual awakening often comes a **deepening connection to nature**. Individuals may find solace and inspiration in the natural world, recognizing its beauty and wisdom. Nature becomes a mirror reflecting the sacredness of existence, reminding individuals of their place within the larger tapestry of life.

Consider the experience of **Sofia**, a city dweller who felt disconnected from the natural world. After embarking on her spiritual journey, she began to seek refuge in local parks and gardens. Each time she immersed herself in nature, Sofia felt a profound sense of peace wash over her. The rustling leaves, the vibrant flowers, and the songs of birds filled her heart with joy.

Through her connection to nature, Sofia realized that the natural world is not separate from her; it is an extension of her being. This awareness deepened her understanding of interconnectedness, igniting a desire to protect and preserve the environment for future generations.

Embracing the Journey

As we explore the signs of spiritual awakening, it is essential to recognize that this journey is not linear. Awakening unfolds uniquely for each individual, shaped by their experiences, beliefs, and readiness. Embracing the process means honoring the ups and downs, the moments of clarity and confusion, and the ebbs and flows of growth.

Ultimately, spiritual awakening invites individuals to live authentically and intentionally, aligning their actions with their true selves. It encourages them to embrace their unique journeys, celebrate their progress, and cultivate compassion for themselves and others.

As we witness the signs of awakening in ourselves and those around us, let us remember that each step taken on this sacred path is an invitation to deepen our connection to the divine. Whether it is through moments of discontent, heightened awareness, emotional release, or compassion, the journey of awakening serves as a reminder of the beauty and richness of life.

Conclusion: The Awakening Continues

In conclusion, spiritual awakening is a profound and transformative journey marked by a myriad of signs and experiences. From the initial discontent of the soul to the emergence of compassion and connection, each step along the way reveals the intricate tapestry of existence.

As individuals navigate the layers of awakening, they are reminded that they are part of a larger cosmic dance—a divine play that unfolds in mysterious and beautiful ways. The signs of awakening serve as beacons of hope, guiding individuals toward a deeper understanding of themselves and their place in the universe.

As we honor our journeys and the journeys of others, may we celebrate the awakening that lies within each of us. Together, let us embrace the magic of life, recognizing that the path to awakening is not a destination but a continuous unfolding—a journey that invites us to explore, connect, and discover the profound truth of our existence.

- **Techniques for recognizing and transcending illusion**

In the vast journey of spiritual awakening, one of the most crucial tasks is to recognize and transcend the **illusions** that cloud our perception of reality. These illusions, rooted in fear, ignorance, and societal conditioning, create a veil that obscures our true nature and keeps us trapped in a cycle of suffering. However, through dedicated practice and inner exploration, we can learn techniques that help us peel away these layers of illusion, revealing the radiant essence of our being.

As we embark on this exploration, we will weave together stories of individuals who have traversed this path, illuminating the techniques that facilitated their transformation. Each tale serves as a guide, offering insights and practical wisdom for recognizing and transcending the illusions that bind us.

The Power of Mindfulness

At the heart of recognizing illusion lies the practice of **mindfulness**. Mindfulness involves bringing awareness to the present moment, observing thoughts, feelings, and sensations without judgment. By cultivating mindfulness, we begin to witness the transient nature of our thoughts and emotions, recognizing that they are not our true selves.

Imagine **Kiran**, a busy entrepreneur overwhelmed by the demands of his career. Caught in the whirlwind of daily tasks, Kiran often found himself reacting to stress and anxiety without pause. One day, a friend introduced him to mindfulness meditation. Initially skeptical, Kiran decided to give it a try.

Sitting quietly, he focused on his breath, noticing the rise and fall of his chest. As thoughts of deadlines and responsibilities flooded his mind, he observed them as fleeting clouds in the vast sky of his consciousness. This simple practice allowed Kiran to detach from the overwhelming narrative of his life, creating space for clarity and calm.

Through mindfulness, Kiran began to recognize the patterns of thought that had kept him trapped in illusion. He realized that his identity was not solely defined by his achievements or failures but was rooted in a deeper sense of self—one that was ever-present and unchanging.

Self-Inquiry and Reflection

Another powerful technique for transcending illusion is **self-inquiry**. This practice involves questioning the assumptions and beliefs that shape our perceptions. By turning our gaze inward, we can uncover the roots of our illusions and challenge the narratives that keep us imprisoned.

Consider the journey of **Rohan**, a young man who struggled with feelings of unworthiness. Despite his many accomplishments, he constantly compared himself to others, feeling inadequate in their presence. Seeking answers, Rohan delved into self-inquiry, asking himself probing questions: "Who am I beyond my achievements?" "What beliefs underpin my feelings of inadequacy?"

As Rohan explored these questions, he began to uncover the deep-seated beliefs instilled in him during childhood—messages of not being enough, not fitting in. Through this process, he learned to challenge these narratives, reframing them into affirmations of self-worth and acceptance.

Self-inquiry allowed Rohan to peel away the layers of illusion that clouded his perception of himself. He recognized that his worthiness was not contingent upon external validation but inherent to his being. This realization became a catalyst for profound change, empowering him to embrace his true self without fear of comparison.

The Role of Breath and Movement

Breathwork and **movement** are essential tools for transcending illusion. The breath is a bridge between the mind and body, serving as an anchor to the present moment. When we consciously engage with our breath, we can release tension, center ourselves, and connect with our inner wisdom.

Take the story of **Aditi**, a woman who had long struggled with anxiety. Seeking relief, she discovered the transformative power of breathwork. By practicing deep, intentional breathing, Aditi learned to calm her racing thoughts and ground herself in the present.

In moments of overwhelm, Aditi would close her eyes, inhale deeply, and exhale slowly, visualizing her fears dissipating with each breath. This simple technique provided her with a sense of agency over her emotional landscape, allowing her to transcend the illusions of panic and fear that had controlled her life.

Additionally, Aditi found solace in movement—yoga and dance became sacred expressions of her spirit. Through the fluidity of movement, she released pent-up energy and emotions, allowing her to reconnect with her body and intuition. This integration of breath and movement became a powerful practice for recognizing the illusions that had held her captive.

Cultivating Compassion and Forgiveness

The practice of **compassion** and **forgiveness** serves as a profound antidote to the illusions of separation and judgment. When we cultivate compassion for ourselves and others, we transcend the barriers that keep us locked in the cycle of illusion.

Consider the experience of **Raj**, a man burdened by anger toward a family member who had wronged him. This anger consumed him, clouding his perception of the relationship and distorting his reality. Realizing he could no longer carry this weight, Raj embarked on a journey of forgiveness.

Through journaling and reflection, Raj explored the emotions tied to his anger. He recognized that holding onto resentment only perpetuated his suffering and kept him locked in a state of illusion. As he practiced compassion toward himself and his family member, he began to understand the complexity of their experiences and the shared humanity that connected them.

Through this process, Raj learned that forgiveness does not condone harmful behavior but liberates the heart from the chains of anger and judgment. This practice allowed him to transcend the illusion of separation, embracing a deeper sense of love and understanding for himself and others.

Embracing Stillness and Silence

In our fast-paced world, the practice of embracing **stillness** and **silence** becomes increasingly vital for recognizing and transcending illusion. In moments of quietude, we can connect with our inner selves, stripping away the distractions of the external world.

Imagine **Sofia**, a woman who had always been busy—her schedule filled with work, social events, and responsibilities. One day, she decided to retreat into nature, seeking solace in the stillness of the mountains. Sitting by a serene lake, Sofia closed her eyes and allowed herself to simply be.

In the silence, she encountered the whispers of her soul—longing for peace, connection, and authenticity. This experience of stillness became a profound reminder of the importance of slowing down and tuning into the essence of who she was.

Through this practice, Sofia began to recognize the illusions that had kept her caught in the whirlwind of life. She realized that true fulfillment comes not from constant busyness but from being present with herself and nurturing her inner landscape.

Connecting with Community

The journey of recognizing and transcending illusion can often feel isolating. However, connecting with a **community** of like-minded individuals provides invaluable support and encouragement. Sharing experiences, insights, and practices with others fosters a sense of belonging and reminds us that we are not alone in our struggles.

Consider the story of **Meera**, who felt a deep calling toward spirituality but struggled to find her place in a world that often dismissed such pursuits. After attending a local meditation group, Meera discovered a community of seekers who resonated with her journey.

In this supportive environment, Meera shared her challenges and breakthroughs, receiving encouragement and guidance from others. The communal experience of meditation and reflection deepened her practice, helping her recognize the illusions that had once clouded her perception.

Through connection, Meera learned that the path of awakening is not a solitary endeavor; it is a shared journey that thrives on the wisdom and support of others. This realization ignited her passion for fostering community, leading her to create spaces where others could explore their own spiritual paths.

Seeking Guidance from Mentors and Teachers

In the quest for recognizing and transcending illusion, seeking **guidance** from mentors and spiritual teachers can be transformative. These individuals offer wisdom, support, and insights that illuminate the path and provide valuable tools for navigating the complexities of awakening.

Take the journey of **Dev**, a young man who felt lost in the chaos of life. He yearned for deeper understanding but struggled to find his way. One day, he encountered a wise teacher who spoke of the nature of illusion and the importance of inner work.

Inspired by this encounter, Dev began to study under the guidance of his mentor, participating in workshops, retreats, and one-on-one sessions. Through their teachings, he learned techniques for recognizing his patterns of thought, releasing limiting beliefs, and cultivating a deeper connection with his true self.

The mentorship provided Dev with the support and accountability he needed to navigate his journey. He discovered that the path to transcending illusion is often illuminated by the wisdom of those who have walked the path before him. This guidance became a beacon of light, helping him stay focused and inspired on his journey.

Practicing Gratitude

The practice of **gratitude** serves as a powerful tool for recognizing and transcending illusion. When we cultivate a sense of gratitude, we shift our focus from what is lacking in our lives to what is abundant and beautiful. This shift in perspective opens our hearts and minds, allowing us to transcend the illusions of scarcity and limitation.

Imagine the experience of **Nisha**, a young woman who had long felt trapped in a cycle of negative thinking. Frustrated with her circumstances, she decided to start a gratitude journal, committing to write down three things she was grateful for each day.

At first, Nisha struggled to find positive aspects in her life. However, as she persisted, she began to notice the small joys—a warm cup of tea, a friend's laughter, the beauty of a sunset. This practice shifted her perspective, enabling her to see the abundance surrounding her.

Through gratitude, Nisha recognized that the illusions of scarcity and inadequacy were merely constructs of her mind. By acknowledging the richness of her experiences, she transcended the limiting beliefs that had once held her captive.

Conclusion: Embracing the Journey of Awakening

As we delve into the techniques for recognizing and transcending illusion, we come to understand that this journey is not a destination but an ongoing process. Each technique, whether it be mindfulness, self-inquiry, breathwork, or connection with community, serves as a stepping stone toward deeper awareness and authenticity.

The stories of Kiran, Rohan, Aditi, Raj, Sofia, Meera, Dev, and Nisha illuminate the diverse paths of awakening. Each individual faced their unique challenges, yet they discovered that the techniques for transcending illusion resonate universally.

In embracing these practices, we empower ourselves to navigate the complexities of existence with grace and clarity. We learn to recognize the illusions that obscure our true nature, revealing the radiant essence of who we are.

As we continue on this journey, let us remember that awakening is not a linear process. It is a dance of exploration, a sacred play of discovering ourselves amidst the layers of illusion. Each step taken brings us closer to the truth, inviting us to embrace the fullness of life with open hearts and open minds.

In this journey of awakening, may we honor ourselves, support one another, and celebrate the beauty of existence, recognizing that we are all interconnected in this divine tapestry of life.

- **The significance of self-inquiry and mindfulness**

In the realm of spiritual awakening, two essential practices stand as pillars of transformation: **self-inquiry** and **mindfulness**. These techniques, deeply intertwined, invite us to embark on an inner journey of exploration, revealing the truths that lie beneath the layers of illusion we have constructed throughout our lives. Through self-inquiry, we learn to question the very fabric of our beliefs, while mindfulness helps us cultivate an awareness of the present moment, allowing us to experience life with clarity and authenticity.

As we delve into this chapter, we will weave together stories of individuals who have embraced these practices, illuminating their significance in the journey of self-discovery. Each narrative serves as a testament to the profound impact that self-inquiry and mindfulness can have on our lives.

The Awakening of Kiran: A Journey of Self-Inquiry

Let us begin with the story of **Kiran**, a successful corporate executive who seemed to have it all—prestige, wealth, and social status. Yet, beneath the veneer of success lay a persistent sense of discontent. Despite achieving his professional goals, Kiran felt a nagging emptiness that he couldn't quite articulate.

One evening, feeling particularly restless, Kiran stumbled upon a book on spirituality that emphasized the importance of self-inquiry. Intrigued, he began to explore the practice, dedicating time each day to ask himself probing questions: "Who am I beyond my job title?" "What are the beliefs that shape my identity?" "What truly brings me joy?"

At first, the questions felt daunting, and Kiran found himself confronted with the uncomfortable truths he had long buried. He discovered that much of his self-worth had been tied to external validation and societal expectations. However, as he continued this practice, Kiran realized that the answers lay not in the accolades he had collected but in a deeper understanding of his true self.

Through self-inquiry, Kiran peeled back the layers of his identity, revealing a profound sense of purpose that transcended material success. He recognized that he was a creative soul yearning for connection and authenticity. This realization catalyzed a transformation, prompting him to shift his career focus towards meaningful work that aligned with his passions.

The Dance of Mindfulness: Sofia's Awakening

Next, we turn to **Sofia**, a young woman who had always lived in a state of anxiety and overwhelm. Juggling work, relationships, and societal expectations, she often felt like she was merely going through the motions of life. One day, a close friend introduced her to mindfulness meditation, sparking a curiosity within her.

Initially hesitant, Sofia decided to attend a mindfulness workshop, hoping to find relief from her stress. Guided by a compassionate instructor, she learned to bring her attention to the present moment, observing her thoughts and feelings without judgment. During these sessions, she discovered the beauty of simply being—of tuning into her breath, the sensations in her body, and the sounds around her.

As Sofia practiced mindfulness daily, she experienced a gradual shift in her perception of reality. The swirling chaos of her thoughts began to settle, revealing a calmness she had never known before. Through this practice, she learned to observe her emotions as passing clouds rather than defining her identity. Each breath became a reminder that she could return to the present, releasing the burdens of the past and the anxieties of the future.

One pivotal moment came when Sofia found herself facing a challenging situation at work. Rather than succumbing to her usual pattern of anxiety, she paused, took a deep breath, and anchored herself in mindfulness. This simple act of presence empowered her to respond with clarity and composure, transforming a potential crisis into an opportunity for growth.

The Intersection of Self-Inquiry and Mindfulness

As we journey further, we come to understand how self-inquiry and mindfulness beautifully complement each other. While self-inquiry allows us to delve into the depths of our beliefs and motivations, mindfulness cultivates the awareness necessary to observe these insights without attachment. Together, they form a powerful framework for personal transformation.

Let us explore the story of **Rohan**, a man who had spent years grappling with self-doubt and negative self-talk. After attending a retreat focused on self-inquiry, Rohan returned home with a newfound commitment to explore the beliefs that had shaped his identity. He began to ask himself questions like, "What fears are driving my actions?" and "What would my life look like if I fully embraced my worth?"

At the same time, Rohan embraced mindfulness as a daily practice. He started each morning with a few minutes of meditation, allowing himself to observe his thoughts without judgment. This practice created a foundation of awareness, helping him to identify the recurring patterns of self-criticism that plagued him.

Through the combination of self-inquiry and mindfulness, Rohan began to unravel the illusion of unworthiness that had held him captive. He recognized that many of his fears were rooted in past experiences rather than objective truths. This realization, paired with the mindfulness practice of observing his thoughts, enabled him to challenge those beliefs and replace them with affirmations of self-love and acceptance.

The Power of Questions: A Journey Within

At the core of self-inquiry lies the power of asking the right questions. These questions act as keys that unlock the door to our inner landscape, revealing the truths that have been obscured by conditioning and illusion.

Let's look at **Meera**, a college student navigating the pressures of academic success and societal expectations. Feeling lost amidst the demands of her studies, she began exploring self-inquiry as a means of understanding her motivations and desires.

Meera set aside time each week to engage in reflective journaling, posing questions such as: "What do I truly want from my life?" "What passions ignite my spirit?" "How do societal expectations shape my choices?"

Through this practice, she unearthed a profound realization: her dreams of pursuing art had been suppressed by the belief that she needed to conform to a more traditional career path. By writing freely and honestly, Meera not only discovered her true passions but also began to cultivate the courage to pursue them.

Simultaneously, she incorporated mindfulness into her routine. Whenever she felt overwhelmed by academic pressures, Meera would take a moment to breathe deeply, returning to the present. This practice of grounding herself allowed her to navigate the demands of her studies with greater ease, reminding her that she was not defined by external achievements but by her unique journey.

The Ripple Effect: Transformation Beyond Self

As individuals like Kiran, Sofia, Rohan, and Meera embraced the practices of self-inquiry and mindfulness, the impact of their transformations extended beyond themselves. Their newfound clarity and authenticity began to ripple into their relationships, careers, and communities.

Kiran, once driven solely by ambition, now approached his work with a sense of purpose and compassion. He fostered a culture of collaboration and creativity in his team, inspiring others to pursue their passions and align their work with their values.

Sofia, filled with gratitude for her mindfulness practice, began leading meditation sessions for friends and colleagues, sharing the tools that had transformed her life. Through her guidance, others discovered the beauty of presence, fostering deeper connections and reducing stress within their community.

Rohan, empowered by his journey of self-inquiry, became an advocate for mental health awareness. He shared his story with vulnerability, encouraging others to confront their fears and embrace their worthiness. Through workshops and speaking engagements, Rohan inspired countless individuals to embark on their paths of self-discovery.

Meera, fueled by her artistic passion, organized community art events that celebrated creativity and self-expression. Through these gatherings, she created spaces for individuals to explore their talents, fostering a sense of belonging and encouragement.

Conclusion: The Journey Continues

As we reflect on the significance of self-inquiry and mindfulness, we recognize that these practices are not merely tools for personal growth; they are profound invitations to awaken to the fullness of life. Through self-inquiry, we unravel the narratives that have shaped our identities, while mindfulness grounds us in the present moment, allowing us to experience life with clarity and grace.

The stories of Kiran, Sofia, Rohan, and Meera remind us that the journey of self-discovery is deeply transformative, impacting not only our lives but also the lives of those around us. Each individual's awakening serves as a beacon of hope, illustrating the power of embracing authenticity and presence.

In the dance of self-inquiry and mindfulness, we find liberation from the constraints of illusion, revealing the beauty of our true selves. As we continue to explore these practices, may we honor our journeys and the journeys of others, celebrating the interconnectedness of our experiences.

Ultimately, the significance of self-inquiry and mindfulness lies in their ability to awaken us to the truth of who we are—radiant beings of consciousness, intricately woven into the fabric of existence. As we embark on this journey together, let us embrace the path of awakening, recognizing that each moment is an opportunity to connect with our true selves and the world around us.

Chapter 6: Harnessing the Power of Yogamaya

- **Practical applications of Yogamaya in daily life**

In the ancient scriptures, **Yogamaya** is described as the divine, mystical power of illusion controlled by the Supreme Being, a manifestation of **Maya** that is not simply a force of delusion but a purposeful, intelligent energy used to orchestrate the cosmic drama of existence. Unlike **Mahamaya**, which binds individuals to the material world, Yogamaya is a subtler and more profound form of divine power that helps spiritual seekers align with the higher truths of existence. It is a spiritual tool rather than a barrier, a means to facilitate one's understanding of the cosmic order and navigate through life with divine awareness.

To understand and harness the power of Yogamaya in daily life is not merely an esoteric pursuit for saints or mystics but a practical approach that can empower any individual seeking spiritual clarity, inner peace, and harmony with the world. Yogamaya invites us to see beyond the illusions that cloud our understanding, enabling us to act with wisdom and purpose while remaining in the world. This chapter explores how the principles of Yogamaya can be applied to transform everyday experiences into opportunities for spiritual growth.

Yogamaya: The Divine Force of Alignment

Yogamaya can be thought of as the divine energy that aligns our human experiences with the cosmic will. It is the energy of **connection**—connecting the finite with the infinite, the individual soul (**Atman**) with the universal soul (**Brahman**). Unlike Mahamaya, which often traps us in cycles of desire, attachment, and ego-driven action, Yogamaya has the power to lift us beyond these confines, guiding us toward spiritual insight and liberation while we continue to engage in the world.

In the **Bhagavad Gita**, Lord Krishna speaks of Yogamaya when explaining how he manifests in the world while remaining unattached and free from the influences of the material realm. He tells Arjuna that he descends into the material plane through the workings of Yogamaya, retaining his divine nature. In this sense, Yogamaya is a bridge between the human and the divine, allowing individuals to perform their duties, live their lives, and yet remain rooted in higher consciousness.

But how does this concept of Yogamaya translate into our daily lives? How can we tap into this divine energy in a practical, meaningful way?

Living with Awareness: Seeing Through the Veil of Illusion

The first step in harnessing the power of Yogamaya is cultivating **awareness**. Much of our suffering and confusion in life stems from our inability to see things as they truly are. We are often caught in the web of perceptions, conditioned by past experiences, societal norms, and personal desires. The mind, when left unchecked, spins endless narratives about the world, reinforcing illusions that keep us locked in the cycle of **Samsara**—the wheel of birth, death, and rebirth.

Yogamaya teaches us to see beyond these illusions. To begin this journey, we must first become conscious of the thoughts, emotions, and perceptions that shape our experience. This can be achieved through **mindfulness**—the practice of observing our mental and emotional states without judgment. By being present in each moment, we can start to disentangle ourselves from automatic reactions and habitual patterns, creating space for a deeper understanding of reality.

For example, when confronted with a difficult situation—be it a challenging relationship, a financial crisis, or a health issue—our typical response is to react out of fear, anger, or anxiety. These emotional reactions are the result of Maya clouding our perception, making us believe that the external situation has power over our inner peace. Yogamaya, however, allows us to approach such situations with **clarity** and **detachment**. Instead of being overwhelmed by the external circumstances, we can step back and recognize that the true source of peace and strength lies within us. By observing the situation from a higher perspective, we can make decisions that are aligned with our spiritual purpose rather than being driven by fleeting emotions.

The Power of Surrender: Trusting the Divine Plan

One of the most powerful aspects of Yogamaya is its ability to guide us toward surrender. In a world governed by Mahamaya, we often cling to the idea of control—we want to control outcomes, other people's actions, and even the flow of life itself. This constant striving for control leads to tension, frustration, and disappointment because the world is inherently unpredictable and ever-changing.

Yogamaya, on the other hand, invites us to surrender to the **divine plan**. This does not mean giving up or resigning ourselves to fate, but rather trusting that there is a higher intelligence at work in the universe, and that everything is unfolding according to divine will. When we learn to surrender, we release the need to micromanage our lives and instead flow with the current of life's events, trusting that whatever happens is ultimately for our spiritual growth.

For instance, when faced with a setback—such as a failed project, a broken relationship, or a health challenge—our immediate reaction is often one of resistance and frustration. We ask, "Why is this happening to me?" But through the lens of Yogamaya, we can shift this perspective. Instead of seeing the setback as an obstacle, we begin to see it as part of the divine plan, an opportunity for growth, learning, and transformation. This attitude of **trust** and **surrender** brings peace, even in the midst of turmoil.

Detachment in Action: The Art of Karma Yoga

Yogamaya also teaches us the importance of **detachment** in action, which is the essence of **Karma Yoga**, or the path of selfless action. In our daily lives, we are constantly engaged in activities—work, relationships, responsibilities, and so on. Most of the time, these actions are driven by a desire for certain results—success, recognition, wealth, or personal fulfillment. But when our happiness depends on these outcomes, we become attached to them, and this attachment binds us to the wheel of Samsara.

Karma Yoga, as illuminated by the teachings of Yogamaya, offers a different approach. It encourages us to perform our duties without attachment to the results, recognizing that the outcomes are ultimately in the hands of the divine. By focusing on the action itself rather than the fruits of the action, we can free ourselves from the bondage of desire and ego. This is not a passive acceptance of fate but a dynamic engagement with life, where we do our best while remaining detached from the results.

Imagine working on a project at your job or home. Normally, you might be concerned about how the project will be received, whether it will bring praise or criticism, success or failure. This concern often creates stress and anxiety, pulling us deeper into illusion. But by applying the principle of Yogamaya, you can approach the project with **equanimity**. You give your best effort, but you are not attached to how others will perceive it or whether it will lead to success. You trust that whatever the outcome, it is part of the divine plan and will serve your highest good.

Balancing Material and Spiritual Life: The Dance of the Two Worlds

Yogamaya teaches us how to navigate the **balance** between the material and spiritual dimensions of life. Many spiritual seekers struggle with the tension between their worldly responsibilities and their inner quest for higher truth. They feel torn between the demands of family, work, and society, and their desire for spiritual growth. But Yogamaya shows us that the material and spiritual worlds are not mutually exclusive; they are interconnected, and our spiritual growth can occur within the context of our everyday lives.

The key lies in **integrating** our spiritual awareness into our daily activities. Yogamaya helps us see that every action, no matter how mundane, can become a form of worship if done with the right attitude. Whether you are cooking a meal, caring for a loved one, or working at your job, these actions can be infused with divine consciousness. By offering every action to the divine, you transform the material world into a playground for spiritual growth.

Take, for instance, the act of cooking. In a purely material sense, cooking is just a physical task—preparing food for nourishment. But when approached with the spirit of Yogamaya, cooking becomes a **sacred ritual**. You recognize that the food you prepare is an offering to the divine presence within yourself and others. Each ingredient, each motion of the hand, becomes imbued with love and devotion. This shifts the experience from a mundane chore to a spiritual practice.

Compassion and Selfless Service: Expanding Beyond the Ego

Yogamaya also opens our hearts to the power of **compassion** and **selfless service**. In the world of Mahamaya, our actions are often driven by self-interest—what we can gain, how we can protect or advance ourselves. But Yogamaya reveals the deeper truth of interconnectedness. It shows us that we are not separate individuals, but part of the larger web of life, and that true happiness comes from serving others with love and compassion.

In daily life, this can manifest in many ways—helping a neighbor in need, offering a kind word to someone who is struggling, or simply listening with an open heart. Through selfless service, we transcend the ego and tap into the divine energy of Yogamaya, which flows through us as love and compassion for all beings. By serving others, we serve the divine, and in doing so, we align ourselves with the cosmic order.

Conclusion: A Life Lived in the Light of Yogamaya

To harness the power of Yogamaya in daily life is to live with greater awareness, surrender, and alignment with the divine. It is to see beyond the surface of things, recognizing that the world of form and action is a sacred dance orchestrated by divine intelligence. Every moment, every experience becomes an opportunity for spiritual growth, a chance to align with the higher truths of existence.

Through Yogamaya, we learn to live in the world without being bound by it, to act without attachment, and to love without expectation. We become instruments of the divine will, channels through which the cosmic energy flows, bringing light, love, and wisdom into the world. In this way, our daily lives become a spiritual journey, where the mundane and the sacred merge, and every action becomes an expression of divine grace.

- Meditative practices for connecting with Yogamaya

In the vast tapestry of spiritual exploration, few concepts resonate as deeply as **Yogamaya**. Often described as the divine feminine energy that veils the true nature of reality, Yogamaya represents the playful and mysterious aspect of the divine, guiding seekers through the labyrinth of illusion towards enlightenment. To connect with this sacred energy, one can engage in various **meditative practices** that cultivate awareness, presence, and harmony with the divine play of existence.

In this chapter, we will journey through the lives of several individuals who embarked on their quests to connect with Yogamaya through meditation. Each story serves as a guiding light, illuminating the significance of these practices in revealing the beauty and wisdom inherent in the fabric of reality.

The Power of Visualization: Kiran's Experience

Let us begin with **Kiran**, a devoted seeker who found himself intrigued by the concept of Yogamaya during his studies of ancient scriptures. He often felt an inexplicable longing to connect with the divine feminine aspect of the universe, yet he struggled to find a pathway to that connection. One day, while meditating, Kiran decided to explore the practice of **visualization** as a means of connecting with Yogamaya.

Sitting in a comfortable position, he closed his eyes and took several deep breaths, allowing himself to settle into a tranquil state. As he inhaled deeply, Kiran envisioned a radiant light enveloping him—a soft, shimmering glow that symbolized the essence of Yogamaya. This light filled the space around him, pulsating with warmth and love.

As Kiran continued to visualize this divine light, he imagined it flowing through him, illuminating every corner of his being. He visualized Yogamaya as a compassionate and nurturing figure, her presence enveloping him in an embrace of love and acceptance. In this sacred space, Kiran felt the illusion of separateness dissolve, replaced by a profound sense of unity with the divine.

With each breath, Kiran repeated affirmations that resonated with his heart: "I am one with the divine play," "Yogamaya guides me toward my true self," and "I am loved, supported, and nurtured." Through this practice of visualization, Kiran not only deepened his connection with Yogamaya but also fostered a greater sense of peace and purpose in his life.

Breathwork: The Flow of Prana with Aditi

Next, we encounter **Aditi**, a young woman seeking to cultivate a deeper relationship with Yogamaya. She had heard stories of how breathwork could connect individuals with the divine, and she felt drawn to explore this practice. Intrigued by the idea that her breath could serve as a bridge to higher consciousness, Aditi set aside time each day for **breath-focused meditation**.

Finding a quiet space in her home, Aditi sat comfortably and closed her eyes. She began by taking deep, intentional breaths, allowing her mind to settle. As she inhaled, she envisioned the life force energy—**prana**—flowing into her body, filling her with vitality and clarity. With each exhale, she imagined releasing any tension, doubt, or negativity, creating space for divine connection.

During her breathwork sessions, Aditi consciously directed her breath toward her heart center, visualizing a warm light expanding with each inhalation. This light represented Yogamaya, the essence of love and nurturing. With every exhale, she surrendered her worries to the universe, trusting that she was held in the embrace of divine grace.

Over time, Aditi noticed profound changes within herself. As she practiced breathwork daily, she became more attuned to the rhythms of life and the energy of Yogamaya flowing through her. In moments of uncertainty, Aditi would turn to her breath, grounding herself in the present moment and inviting the divine presence of Yogamaya to guide her actions.

The Dance of Movement: Meera's Exploration

Meera was an artist who had always felt a deep connection to the rhythms of life. Yet, as she navigated the challenges of adulthood, she often lost touch with her creative spirit. Inspired by the idea that movement could connect her to Yogamaya, she began exploring **dance as a form of meditation**.

Meera created a sacred space in her studio, adorned with soft lighting and calming music. She allowed herself to move freely, letting her body express what was held within. With each movement, she focused on the sensations in her body, allowing herself to surrender to the flow of energy.

As she danced, Meera envisioned Yogamaya guiding her movements, her energy enveloping her like a gentle breeze. In this state of surrender, she felt her creativity blossoming, and her artistic expressions began to mirror the divine play of the universe.

The practice of dance became a form of prayer for Meera. Each movement was an offering to Yogamaya, a celebration of life's beauty and intricacies. Through this practice, she discovered that connecting with the divine feminine was not confined to stillness; it was an energetic dance—a celebration of existence itself.

Chanting and Mantra: Rohan's Connection

Rohan, a young man deeply immersed in spiritual study, sought to deepen his connection with Yogamaya through the practice of **chanting and mantra meditation**. Inspired by the power of sound to elevate consciousness, Rohan dedicated himself to chanting sacred mantras that resonated with the essence of Yogamaya.

Each morning, Rohan would rise before dawn, finding solace in the quietude of the early hours. He would sit in a comfortable position, focusing on his breath, and then begin to chant the mantra "**Om Shakti**," which represents the divine feminine energy of creation.

As Rohan repeated the mantra, he felt the vibrations reverberate through his entire being, awakening the dormant energy within him. Each repetition became a bridge, connecting him to the sacred energy of Yogamaya. He envisioned the mantra enveloping him in a cocoon of light, allowing him to surrender his ego and tap into the essence of the divine.

With every chant, Rohan experienced a profound sense of connection, as if Yogamaya were dancing through his words and intentions. This practice of mantra became a source of strength and empowerment, reminding him of the transformative power of the divine feminine.

Nature as a Sacred Space: Raj's Revelation

Raj was a nature lover who often sought refuge in the outdoors. He believed that connecting with nature was a pathway to experiencing Yogamaya's essence. Inspired by this belief, Raj began to engage in **nature meditation** as a way to immerse himself in the divine play of existence.

On weekends, he ventured into the nearby forest, allowing the beauty of nature to surround him. As he found a quiet spot beneath a tree, he closed his eyes and took a moment to listen to the sounds of the forest—the rustling leaves, the chirping birds, and the gentle breeze.

In this sacred space, Raj felt a profound sense of unity with the world around him. He visualized Yogamaya as the energy flowing through every leaf, every creature, and every ray of sunlight. This connection reminded him that he was not separate from the universe; he was an integral part of its dance.

With each breath, Raj inhaled the fresh air, feeling it fill him with vitality and joy. As he exhaled, he surrendered any feelings of fear or disconnection, trusting in the wisdom of the universe. This practice in nature became a celebration of life's interconnectedness, allowing Raj to experience the divine in every moment.

Creating Rituals of Connection

As our journey continues, we learn that the practices of connecting with Yogamaya can be enhanced through the creation of **rituals**. These rituals serve as sacred ceremonies that honor the divine feminine and invite its presence into our lives.

Consider **Sofia**, who sought to deepen her connection with Yogamaya by creating a monthly ritual of honoring the cycles of the moon. Each full moon, she gathered with friends to celebrate their connection to the divine. They would light candles, create altars adorned with flowers, and share intentions for the month ahead.

During these gatherings, Sofia led her friends in guided meditations, inviting them to connect with the energy of Yogamaya. They would visualize the moonlight enveloping them, awakening their intuition and nurturing their spirits. In this sacred space, they experienced the beauty of sisterhood and the divine feminine energy flowing through their gathering.

Through these rituals, Sofia and her friends discovered a profound sense of community and support. They celebrated each other's journeys and cultivated a shared understanding of the importance of connecting with Yogamaya as a source of strength and inspiration.

The Integration of Practices

As we reflect on the meditative practices for connecting with Yogamaya, we recognize that each individual's journey is unique. The stories of Kiran, Aditi, Meera, Rohan, Raj, and Sofia illustrate the diversity of pathways leading to the divine feminine.

Whether through visualization, breathwork, dance, chanting, nature meditation, or rituals, these practices provide a bridge to connect with the sacred energy of Yogamaya. The common thread woven throughout their experiences is the intention to cultivate awareness, presence, and surrender to the divine play of existence.

In the tapestry of spiritual awakening, connecting with Yogamaya serves as a reminder of the beauty and wisdom that reside within each of us. By engaging in these practices, we honor the divine feminine and invite its presence into our lives, allowing us to navigate the complexities of existence with grace and authenticity.

Conclusion: The Ever-Unfolding Journey

As we conclude this chapter, let us remember that the journey of connecting with Yogamaya is not a destination but an ever-unfolding process. Each practice offers us an opportunity to deepen our understanding of ourselves and our relationship with the universe.

In embracing these meditative practices, we empower ourselves to navigate the layers of illusion, revealing the radiant essence of who we are. Through self-inquiry, breathwork, movement, chanting, and ritual, we open the door to the divine play of existence, inviting the energy of Yogamaya to guide us on our journey.

May we honor our experiences and the experiences of others as we walk this path together. In connecting with Yogamaya, we not only awaken to our true selves but also celebrate the interconnectedness of all beings, recognizing that we are all part of this beautiful dance of life.

- **The art of manifestation and intention setting**

In the realm of human experience, the concept of **manifestation** holds a unique power. It embodies the ability to bring our deepest desires and dreams into reality through focused intention and belief. Yet, the art of manifestation is not merely about wishing for what we want; it is a profound journey of self-discovery, alignment, and collaboration with the universe. This chapter will unfold the stories of individuals who navigated the intricacies of manifestation and intention setting, illustrating the transformative power of these practices.

The Journey of Kiran: Discovering His Heart's Desire

Let us begin with the tale of **Kiran**, a young man who had always felt a calling deep within his heart. Despite achieving conventional success, he felt a sense of emptiness and discontent, as though he were living someone else's life. One day, while wandering through a local bookstore, Kiran stumbled upon a book titled **"The Power of Intention."** Intrigued, he purchased it and devoured its teachings.

The book emphasized the importance of understanding one's true desires before embarking on the journey of manifestation. Kiran was inspired to reflect on his aspirations, seeking clarity about what he truly wanted. He began a daily practice of **journaling**, writing down his dreams and desires with an open heart.

Each evening, he would sit quietly, pen in hand, and ask himself profound questions: "What ignites my soul?" "What legacy do I wish to leave behind?" "How do I want to feel in my life?" As he poured his thoughts onto the pages, Kiran unearthed a long-buried dream of becoming an artist—a passion that had been overshadowed by societal expectations.

With newfound clarity, Kiran realized that to manifest his heart's desire, he needed to set a clear intention. He created a vision board, filling it with images of art supplies, galleries, and quotes that inspired him. Each day, he would spend a few moments visualizing his dream as if it were already his reality. This practice of visualization infused him with energy and excitement, igniting the flame of hope within.

Aditi's Leap of Faith: Aligning with Her Vision

Aditi, a close friend of Kiran's, had also been searching for her purpose in life. She felt a strong desire to create positive change in her community but struggled to find a way to do so. After hearing about Kiran's journey, she decided to explore the art of manifestation herself.

Aditi began by clarifying her intentions. She spent time reflecting on the impact she wanted to make, jotting down her ideas and aspirations. She envisioned herself leading community initiatives that promoted sustainability and social well-being. With her vision clear, she started to practice **affirmations**, positive statements that reinforced her belief in her abilities and potential.

Each morning, Aditi would stand in front of the mirror and declare with conviction, "I am a catalyst for positive change. I attract opportunities that align with my vision." These affirmations became a powerful part of her morning routine, instilling confidence and motivation within her.

One day, while volunteering at a local charity, Aditi met **Raj**, a passionate advocate for environmental sustainability. They connected over their shared vision for creating a better world. Inspired by their conversation, they decided to collaborate on a community garden project, a manifestation of Aditi's intention to promote sustainable living. As they worked together, Aditi witnessed how the universe conspired to align her with the people and resources she needed to bring her vision to life.

Rohan's Experiment: The Power of Gratitude

Meanwhile, **Rohan** had his own journey with manifestation. He was an aspiring writer, struggling with self-doubt and fear of failure. After attending a workshop on intention setting, he felt inspired to implement the principles he had learned. Rohan decided to create a **gratitude journal**, recognizing that gratitude was a powerful force in attracting positive experiences.

Each night, he would write down three things he was grateful for, focusing not only on the external circumstances but also on his inner qualities and strengths. "I am grateful for my creativity," he would write. "I am grateful for my supportive friends." As he cultivated a mindset of gratitude, Rohan noticed a shift in his energy. He began to feel more confident in his writing and found joy in the process rather than fixating on the outcome.

Encouraged by this newfound perspective, Rohan set a clear intention to complete his first novel within a year. He created a structured plan, dedicating time each day to write. He visualized himself holding his published book, feeling the excitement of sharing his story with the world. As he aligned his actions with his intention, opportunities began to arise. He connected with a writing group, received feedback on his work, and ultimately found a publisher for his novel.

The Collective Power of Intention: Meera and Sofia

In another part of the city, **Meera** and **Sofia**, two close friends, embarked on their own manifestation journey together. They had always dreamed of hosting a community art exhibition that showcased local artists. Fueled by their shared passion, they decided to set a collective intention for the event.

The duo began by conducting **visioning sessions**, where they would meditate together, visualizing the exhibition in great detail. They imagined the vibrant artwork adorning the walls, the joyful energy of attendees, and the sense of connection created through art. During these sessions, they focused on the feeling of community and inspiration that they wanted to cultivate.

As they aligned their intention, Meera and Sofia took inspired action. They reached out to local artists, secured a venue, and promoted the event through social media. They practiced affirmations, reminding themselves that they were capable of creating an impactful experience. "Our art exhibition will bring people together and inspire creativity," they would affirm with conviction.

When the day of the exhibition arrived, the energy was electric. Artists and attendees filled the space, connecting and celebrating the beauty of creativity. The event exceeded their expectations, attracting attention from local media and fostering a sense of community that inspired everyone involved. Meera and Sofia realized that by setting a clear intention and collaborating with like-minded individuals, they had manifested their dream into reality.

The Role of Surrender: Nisha's Journey

Nisha had been following the journey of her friends with curiosity. She had always been skeptical of manifestation, believing that hard work alone would determine her fate. However, after witnessing the transformations in her friends, she decided to explore the concept herself.

Nisha's journey began with setting an intention to find her true calling. However, she struggled with the pressure of wanting to control the outcome. As she shared her concerns with Kiran, he gently reminded her of the importance of **surrender** in the manifestation process. He encouraged her to trust in the timing of the universe and remain open to unexpected possibilities.

Inspired by this conversation, Nisha started to practice **letting go**. She created a ritual where she would write down her intentions and then release them into the universe. She would light a candle and silently surrender her desires, trusting that whatever was meant for her would come in its own time.

Over the following weeks, Nisha experienced a sense of relief and freedom. She began to explore new interests without the pressure of achieving specific outcomes. To her surprise, she found herself drawn to a volunteer opportunity at a local organization focused on youth mentorship. Through this experience, Nisha discovered her passion for guiding and supporting young minds.

With time, Nisha embraced the realization that manifestation was not merely about control; it was a dance of intention and surrender, a collaboration with the universe that honored her desires while remaining open to the unexpected.

The Interconnectedness of All: A Collective Journey

As our stories converge, we witness the profound interconnectedness of each individual's journey. Kiran, Aditi, Rohan, Meera, Sofia, and Nisha each navigated their paths with intention and authenticity, discovering that manifestation was not solely a solitary pursuit but a collective journey.

In a celebratory gathering, they came together to share their experiences, recognizing the beauty of their unique journeys while acknowledging the power of collaboration. They discussed how intention setting had transformed their lives, creating a ripple effect that extended beyond their individual desires.

During the gathering, they engaged in a collective **intention-setting ceremony**, each taking turns to articulate their dreams and aspirations aloud. They created a shared vision for their community, envisioning a space filled with creativity, connection, and support. In that moment, they felt the energy of their intentions intertwine, amplifying their collective power.

Conclusion: The Art of Manifestation as a Life Practice

As we conclude this chapter, we reflect on the art of manifestation and intention setting as a dynamic and transformative practice. Through the stories of Kiran, Aditi, Rohan, Meera, Sofia, and Nisha, we witness the diverse pathways to manifesting one's desires and dreams.

The journey of manifestation requires clarity of intention, a willingness to take inspired action, and the courage to surrender to the flow of life. It invites us to explore our desires deeply, understand our motivations, and align ourselves with the universal energy that supports our aspirations.

As we embrace the art of manifestation, let us remember that our desires are not separate from the universe; they are threads woven into the greater tapestry of existence. Each intention we set, each action we take, contributes to the unfolding of our unique journey while influencing the collective consciousness of humanity.

In this sacred dance of manifestation, may we honor our desires, trust in the process, and celebrate the beauty of life as it unfolds. Let us continue to explore the art of manifestation as a lifelong practice, recognizing that we are co-creators in the magnificent tapestry of existence.

Chapter 7: The Role of Grace and Surrender

- **Understanding the concept of divine grace**

In the vast landscape of human experience, few concepts evoke as much intrigue and reverence as **divine grace**. It is often described as an unearned gift from the universe, a force that transcends human understanding and fosters an intimate connection with the divine. To comprehend the essence of divine grace, we must embark on a journey that explores the lives of individuals who encountered its profound impact—transformations that would illuminate their paths toward surrender, acceptance, and profound spiritual awakening.

The Tale of Arjun: A Life of Struggle

Our story begins with **Arjun**, a man whose life was marked by relentless struggle. He grew up in a modest village, where hardship was the norm and dreams often felt like distant stars. His parents toiled daily to provide for their family, instilling in him a strong work ethic but little understanding of the spiritual realm. As a young boy, Arjun was filled with aspirations of a brighter future, yet as he matured, the weight of his responsibilities pressed heavily upon him.

Despite his best efforts, Arjun faced constant obstacles. Jobs were scarce, and opportunities seemed to slip through his fingers like grains of sand. He became consumed by despair, often questioning the purpose of his existence. Yet, beneath the layers of frustration, a flicker of hope still resided within him—a yearning for something greater, a connection to the divine.

One fateful evening, while wandering through the fields, Arjun stumbled upon an elderly man sitting quietly beneath a tree. Intrigued by the man's serene demeanor, he approached him. The old man, sensing Arjun's turmoil, smiled warmly and invited him to sit.

"Tell me, young one," the old man began, "what weighs heavily on your heart?"

Arjun poured out his struggles—the frustration of unfulfilled dreams, the burden of expectations, and the seemingly endless cycle of hardship. As he spoke, the old man listened patiently, his eyes reflecting an understanding that transcended words.

When Arjun finished, the old man shared a simple truth: "Divine grace is always present, even in your darkest moments. It is the unseen hand that guides us, the gentle whisper that reminds us we are not alone."

The Awakening: A Seed of Grace

These words resonated deeply within Arjun, planting a seed of curiosity about the concept of grace. Inspired by the old man's wisdom, he decided to seek a deeper understanding of this divine force. He began to explore spiritual texts and teachings, discovering that grace is not something to be earned but rather a natural state of being—an inherent gift that flows from the universe.

Arjun's journey into spirituality was not without its challenges. He encountered skepticism from those around him, people who viewed his quest for understanding as a distraction from the harsh realities of life. Yet, he pressed on, drawn to the stories of individuals who had experienced profound transformations through surrendering to divine grace.

As he delved deeper, Arjun encountered the teachings of various spiritual leaders who spoke of surrender as a crucial aspect of connecting with grace. They emphasized the importance of releasing control, allowing life to unfold naturally, and trusting that the universe had a greater plan.

The Art of Surrender: The Bridge to Grace

In a moment of quiet reflection, Arjun realized that his life had been marked by an insatiable desire to control every outcome. This desire stemmed from a fear of uncertainty—a fear that had kept him trapped in a cycle of struggle. To embrace grace, he understood, he needed to practice **surrender**.

Surrendering did not mean giving up; rather, it was an invitation to let go of the need for control and to trust in the wisdom of the universe. Inspired, Arjun began to incorporate daily practices of surrender into his life. Each morning, he would sit in stillness, close his eyes, and breathe deeply, envisioning himself releasing his burdens into the cosmic flow.

He would silently repeat affirmations: "I surrender my fears. I trust in divine timing. I am open to the gifts of grace." With each breath, Arjun felt a sense of lightness, as if the weight of the world was slowly lifting off his shoulders.

As days turned into weeks, Arjun noticed a shift within himself. The anxiety that had once consumed him began to dissipate, replaced by a profound sense of peace. He discovered that by surrendering, he opened himself to new possibilities—opportunities that had previously eluded him.

One day, while volunteering at a local community center, he met **Maya**, a passionate social worker dedicated to empowering youth in the village. Their shared values and vision for a better future ignited a spark between them. As they collaborated on various projects, Arjun found himself drawn to her warmth and compassion.

The Role of Grace in Transformation

Maya, too, had her journey with grace. She had faced her own struggles, having grown up in a challenging environment where hope was often overshadowed by despair. Yet, through her experiences, she had cultivated a deep faith in the power of divine grace. She often spoke of how grace had guided her through the toughest of times, providing strength and resilience when she needed it most.

"Grace is like the river that flows beneath the surface," Maya explained to Arjun one afternoon as they took a break from their work. "It is always there, nourishing us even when we can't see it. It teaches us that our struggles are not in vain, and that surrendering allows us to align with a greater purpose."

Arjun listened intently, captivated by her perspective. As he shared his own journey of surrender and discovery, he felt a deep connection blossoming between them. It was as if grace had woven their paths together, guiding them toward a shared vision of creating positive change in their community.

Together, they initiated programs that empowered local youth, teaching them valuable skills and fostering a sense of belonging. Arjun's passion for art found a place in these initiatives, allowing him to express his creativity while uplifting others. The work they did resonated deeply within him, filling the void that had once existed.

The Dance of Grace and Surrender

As Arjun's life blossomed with purpose and connection, he began to understand the intricate dance between grace and surrender. Divine grace is not merely a passive force; it requires an active participation from individuals. It invites us to surrender our fears, doubts, and attachments, creating space for the universe to unfold its blessings.

One evening, as the sun set over the horizon, casting a golden glow across the village, Arjun found himself reflecting on the transformative journey he had undertaken. He sat quietly, feeling a deep sense of gratitude for the grace that had guided him.

In that moment, he realized that surrendering to grace does not mean relinquishing responsibility; rather, it is an act of alignment with the greater flow of life. It is about trusting that the universe conspires in our favor when we let go of the need to control every aspect of our lives.

A Collective Experience of Grace: The Community Celebration

As time passed, Arjun and Maya decided to host a **community celebration**, inviting the villagers to come together in gratitude for the blessings they had received. They organized workshops, art displays, and storytelling sessions, creating an atmosphere of joy and connection.

On the day of the celebration, the village buzzed with excitement. Families gathered, sharing laughter, food, and stories of resilience. Arjun displayed his artwork, capturing the beauty of nature and the essence of human connection. Maya led discussions on the power of grace and surrender, inspiring others to embrace these concepts in their lives.

As the sun dipped below the horizon, casting a warm glow over the gathering, Arjun and Maya stood hand in hand, looking out at the community they had helped uplift. In that moment, they felt a profound sense of gratitude for the journey they had undertaken together—one marked by grace, surrender, and the transformative power of love.

Conclusion: Embracing Grace in Everyday Life

As we conclude this chapter, we are reminded that divine grace is a guiding light illuminating our paths, often when we least expect it. It invites us to embrace surrender, teaching us that we do not have to navigate life's challenges alone. Through the stories of Arjun, Maya, and their community, we witness the profound impact of grace in transforming lives and fostering connection.

In embracing grace, we cultivate a deeper understanding of our purpose, aligning ourselves with the flow of life. It is through surrender that we find liberation from the burdens of control, allowing divine guidance to lead us toward our highest potential.

May we carry these lessons into our own lives, recognizing that grace is always available to us, waiting patiently for our willingness to surrender. In the dance of grace and surrender, we discover the beauty of life's unfolding, the interconnectedness of all beings, and the profound wisdom that resides within our hearts.

- **The importance of surrendering to the flow of life**

In the grand tapestry of life, the concept of **surrender** emerges as a vital thread that weaves through our experiences, challenges, and triumphs. It invites us to release our grip on control, to trust the unfolding journey, and to embrace the natural rhythms of existence. This chapter explores the profound significance of surrendering to the flow of life through the intertwined stories of diverse characters, each navigating their unique paths toward acceptance, peace, and personal transformation.

The Journey of Ravi: A Life of Control

We begin our exploration with **Ravi**, a man whose life was defined by an insatiable need for control. Raised in a family that prioritized success above all else, Ravi was instilled with the belief that hard work and determination were the keys to achieving his dreams. He excelled academically, pursued a lucrative career, and meticulously planned every aspect of his life. However, despite his accomplishments, Ravi felt an underlying sense of anxiety and dissatisfaction.

As he approached his thirtieth birthday, he found himself trapped in a cycle of unfulfilled expectations. The pressure to maintain his meticulously crafted life became overwhelming. Despite his success, he often lay awake at night, plagued by a gnawing sense of emptiness. He felt as though he were swimming against the current, desperately trying to steer his life in a particular direction while ignoring the subtle whispers of his heart.

One evening, feeling particularly lost, Ravi sought refuge at a local café. While sipping his coffee, he overheard a conversation between two elderly women at a nearby table. They spoke of life's unpredictability and the beauty of surrendering to its flow. Intrigued, Ravi listened intently as one of the women shared her own story of transformation.

"I used to plan every detail of my life," she recounted. "But when I learned to surrender, I discovered a new world of possibilities. Life has a way of guiding us if we allow it to."

The Awakening: A Seed of Curiosity

Inspired by the women's conversation, Ravi began to question his own approach to life. What if surrendering to the flow could lead to a deeper sense of fulfillment? The idea lingered in his mind, planting a seed of curiosity.

In the following days, Ravi embarked on a journey of exploration, seeking to understand the concept of surrender more deeply. He delved into books on mindfulness, spirituality, and personal growth, discovering the profound wisdom embedded in the teachings of sages and philosophers throughout history.

Through his reading, Ravi learned that surrender is not an act of weakness but rather a courageous acceptance of the present moment. It is the recognition that life unfolds in its own rhythm, often beyond our limited understanding. He discovered that by surrendering, he could cultivate a sense of trust in the universe and align himself with its natural flow.

As he pondered these ideas, Ravi decided to experiment with the practice of surrender in his daily life. He began by setting aside time each morning to reflect on his intentions, allowing himself to visualize his desires without clinging to rigid outcomes. Instead of forcing specific results, he embraced the possibility that life could surprise him in unexpected ways.

A Transformational Encounter: The Wisdom of Anaya

One afternoon, while attending a local wellness retreat, Ravi met **Anaya**, a gentle soul whose presence exuded warmth and serenity. Anaya had dedicated her life to exploring the art of surrender, and she willingly shared her insights with Ravi.

"Surrendering to the flow of life is like dancing with the universe," she explained, her voice soothing. "It requires us to let go of the need to control and to trust that the universe knows the steps to take."

Intrigued by her analogy, Ravi listened as Anaya described her own journey. She had once been a high-powered executive, consumed by ambition and success, until a series of personal crises shattered her carefully constructed life. It was during this dark period that she discovered the transformative power of surrender.

"After hitting rock bottom, I realized I had been clinging to illusions," Anaya said. "When I let go, I felt the weight lift off my shoulders. I began to trust in the process of life and allow myself to be guided by the flow."

Her words resonated deeply within Ravi, prompting him to reflect on his own fears and attachments. He realized that the anxiety he felt was rooted in his desperate attempts to control every aspect of his life.

Embracing Uncertainty: A Journey of Discovery

As Ravi continued to explore the concept of surrender, he began to practice mindfulness and meditation. Each day, he dedicated time to quiet his mind, allowing thoughts to come and go like leaves floating on a stream. In these moments of stillness, he discovered a profound sense of clarity and peace.

One morning, during a meditation session, Ravi experienced a pivotal moment. As he closed his eyes and focused on his breath, he envisioned himself standing by a river. The water flowed effortlessly, gliding over rocks and branches, adapting to its surroundings. In that moment, he understood: surrendering to life's flow meant trusting that he could navigate the currents, even in the face of uncertainty.

Encouraged by this insight, Ravi decided to take a leap of faith. He let go of his rigid plans and opened himself to new opportunities. He began to engage with life more authentically, embracing spontaneity and adventure. He explored hobbies he had previously dismissed, from painting to hiking, allowing himself to be guided by his passions rather than societal expectations.

The Gift of Letting Go: Ravi's Transformation

As Ravi continued on his journey, he noticed a profound shift in his perspective. The tight grip of anxiety that had once held him captive began to loosen. He found joy in the present moment, savoring life's simple pleasures—a sunset, a shared laugh with friends, or the sound of rain against the window.

Through this newfound sense of freedom, Ravi discovered a deeper connection with others. He fostered relationships based on authenticity rather than expectation, surrounding himself with individuals who encouraged him to embrace his true self.

As the months passed, Ravi realized that surrendering to the flow of life had not only transformed his internal landscape but had also opened doors to unexpected opportunities. He was offered a chance to lead a community art project, combining his passion for creativity with his desire to uplift others.

In the process of sharing his art with the community, Ravi felt a sense of purpose emerge—one that transcended personal ambition. He recognized that by surrendering to the flow of life, he had become a vessel for something greater than himself.

The Interconnectedness of All: A Collective Experience

As Ravi continued to engage with his community, he met other individuals who had also embraced the power of surrender. Among them was **Lila**, a vibrant woman who had overcome her own struggles with control.

Lila shared her story of transformation, describing how she had once been consumed by the desire for perfection in every aspect of her life. After experiencing a series of setbacks, she began to recognize the beauty of imperfection and the importance of letting go. "When I stopped trying to be perfect, I found freedom," she explained. "Embracing the messiness of life allowed me to experience joy in ways I never imagined."

Inspired by Lila's journey, Ravi realized that surrendering to the flow of life not only enhanced his own experience but also fostered a sense of interconnectedness among those around him. Together, they created a space where vulnerability was welcomed, and authenticity flourished.

Through their shared stories and experiences, they formed a community that celebrated the art of surrender, nurturing one another through the ups and downs of life. They organized gatherings, where individuals could express their struggles and triumphs, reinforcing the understanding that surrender was a universal journey.

The Flow of Life: A Dance of Trust

As the seasons changed, Ravi felt a profound sense of gratitude for the lessons he had learned. He understood that surrendering to the flow of life is an ongoing practice—one that requires continuous awareness and trust.

One evening, as Ravi watched the sunset paint the sky in hues of gold and lavender, he reflected on the beauty of existence. He realized that life's journey is not solely about reaching a destination but about embracing the entire experience—the joys, the sorrows, and the unexpected twists and turns.

Surrendering to the flow of life became a dance of trust for Ravi. He understood that while he may not always have control over external circumstances, he could choose how to respond to them. He found comfort in the knowledge that the universe is always conspiring in his favor, guiding him toward growth and discovery.

Conclusion: Embracing the Flow

As we conclude this chapter, we recognize the profound importance of surrendering to the flow of life. Through the stories of Ravi, Anaya, Lila, and their community, we witness the transformative power of letting go and embracing uncertainty.

Surrendering to the flow invites us to release the burdens of control, to trust in the inherent wisdom of life, and to embrace the beauty of the present moment. It is a journey that cultivates resilience, authenticity, and deep connections with ourselves and others.

May we carry these lessons into our own lives, embracing the currents of existence and recognizing that surrendering to the flow is not an endpoint but a continuous journey of discovery and growth. In this dance with life, we find the courage to let go, allowing the universe to guide us toward our true purpose.

- **Case studies of transformative experiences through surrender**

In a world often driven by ambition and the relentless pursuit of control, the concept of **surrender** emerges as a transformative force capable of unlocking profound change. Surrendering does not imply giving up; instead, it represents an invitation to align oneself with the flow of life, to trust in the journey, and to embrace the unexpected. This chapter presents a series of **case studies** illustrating how individuals from diverse backgrounds have experienced transformative shifts through the practice of surrender. These narratives serve as powerful testimonies to the potential for growth, healing, and profound change that can arise when we let go of the need to control every aspect of our lives.

Case Study 1: Sarah's Journey from Burnout to Balance

Background

Sarah, a successful corporate executive in her late thirties, had built a career that many would envy. She was known for her sharp intellect and relentless work ethic, often putting in long hours to climb the corporate ladder. Yet, beneath the surface, Sarah felt increasingly trapped in a cycle of stress and burnout. The pressures of her job left her feeling drained and disconnected from her passions and relationships.

The Turning Point

After suffering a panic attack during a crucial presentation, Sarah recognized that something had to change. That evening, she stumbled upon a local yoga studio hosting a workshop on surrender and mindfulness. Skeptical yet intrigued, she decided to attend, hoping to find some relief from her overwhelming stress.

During the workshop, the instructor spoke about the power of surrender as a means to reclaim balance and well-being. Sarah was introduced to mindfulness practices that encouraged participants to let go of the need for perfection and control. The instructor guided them through a series of breathwork exercises, inviting them to release their worries with each exhale.

The Experience of Surrender

As Sarah participated in the workshop, she experienced a profound moment of clarity. She realized that her constant striving for success had led her to neglect her own well-being. In the quiet of the studio, she allowed herself to feel the weight of her burdens and let go of her need to be in control. She learned to embrace vulnerability, acknowledging that asking for help was not a sign of weakness but rather an essential step toward healing.

From that day forward, Sarah committed to incorporating mindfulness practices into her daily life. She began meditating each morning, focusing on her breath and setting intentions for the day. She also learned to set boundaries at work, prioritizing self-care over relentless ambition.

The Transformation

Over time, Sarah experienced a profound transformation. She discovered newfound balance in her life, allowing herself to pursue activities that brought her joy—such as painting and spending time with family.

By surrendering to the flow of life, she not only regained her well-being but also cultivated deeper connections with her colleagues, fostering a healthier work environment.

As Sarah embraced her journey of surrender, she found that her professional performance improved as well. She learned to approach challenges with a sense of curiosity and openness, rather than fear. Her ability to collaborate and communicate effectively flourished, leading to new opportunities and recognition within her organization.

Case Study 2: Amir's Journey of Healing Through Surrender

Background

Amir, a mid-thirties graphic designer, had struggled with chronic anxiety for most of his adult life. Despite his creative talent, he found it difficult to express himself fully, often succumbing to self-doubt and fear of judgment. His anxiety manifested in various ways, from sleepless nights to panic attacks, hindering his ability to connect with others and pursue his dreams.

The Catalyst for Change

After attending a support group where members shared their experiences with anxiety and mental health, Amir was introduced to the idea of surrendering to his emotions rather than resisting them. One of the group members shared a powerful story about how surrendering to her feelings had led to profound healing.

Intrigued by the concept, Amir decided to explore the practice further. He began to journal about his thoughts and emotions, allowing himself to express his fears without judgment. He realized that much of his anxiety stemmed from his attempts to control his feelings, to fit into a mold that society had created.

The Healing Process

Through his journaling, Amir experienced a breakthrough. He recognized that surrendering did not mean succumbing to his anxiety; instead, it meant acknowledging and accepting it as part of his experience. He learned to create space for his emotions, allowing them to flow through him rather than pushing them away.

In a moment of vulnerability, Amir decided to reach out for help, seeking therapy to navigate his anxiety. His therapist encouraged him to embrace mindfulness practices, teaching him how to ground himself in the present moment. Amir began practicing meditation and breathwork regularly, finding solace in the stillness.

The Transformation

As Amir surrendered to his emotions, he noticed a gradual shift in his perspective. He began to view his anxiety not as an enemy to be fought but as a teacher guiding him toward deeper self-awareness. With each practice of surrender, he felt lighter, more at ease in his own skin.

Emboldened by his healing journey, Amir also began to embrace his creative expression without fear of judgment. He started sharing his artwork on social media, finding a supportive community of fellow artists who resonated with his journey. The act of sharing his creations became a celebration of vulnerability, inspiring others to embrace their own stories.

Through surrendering to his emotions and connecting with his creativity, Amir found a renewed sense of purpose. His art became a channel for healing, both for himself and others, as he expressed the raw beauty of the human experience.

Case Study 3: Linda's Spiritual Awakening Through Surrender

Background

Linda, a retired teacher in her sixties, had spent much of her life dedicated to educating others. However, as she entered retirement, she struggled with a profound sense of loss and purposelessness. The transition left her feeling unanchored, and she often reflected on the dreams and aspirations she had set aside throughout her life.

The Call to Explore

During a visit to a local bookstore, Linda stumbled upon a book about spiritual awakening and the practice of surrender. Intrigued by the idea that surrender could lead to a deeper connection with the universe, she purchased the book and began her journey of exploration.

Through her reading, Linda learned about the power of letting go of attachments and expectations. The author emphasized that surrendering opens the door to a more profound sense of purpose and fulfillment.

The Awakening Experience

Motivated by her newfound insights, Linda began to practice meditation and self-reflection. Each day, she dedicated time to connect with her inner self, allowing her thoughts and feelings to surface without judgment. She sought to uncover her true passions and desires, which had long been buried beneath societal expectations.

One afternoon, as Linda sat in her garden surrounded by vibrant flowers, she experienced a moment of deep clarity. In that serene space, she felt a profound connection to nature and the universe. It was as if the world around her was whispering secrets of beauty and wonder.

In that moment, she understood that surrendering to the flow of life meant letting go of her preconceived notions about herself and embracing the infinite possibilities of existence. She felt liberated, as if she had shed layers of conditioning that had held her back for so long.

The Transformation

Emboldened by her awakening, Linda decided to pursue her lifelong passion for painting, something she had always wanted to do but had never allowed herself the time. She enrolled in an art class, embracing her creativity with childlike wonder. Through each stroke of the brush, she surrendered to the process, discovering joy in expressing herself authentically.

As Linda continued her journey, she also sought to connect with others who shared her passions. She began organizing art workshops in her community, inviting others to explore their creativity without judgment. In these gatherings, she witnessed the power of surrender in action, as participants let go of self-doubt and embraced their artistic expression.

Through her journey of surrender, Linda not only rediscovered her passions but also found a sense of purpose in uplifting others. Her art became a vehicle for connection and healing, and she felt deeply fulfilled in her role as a mentor to aspiring artists.

Conclusion: The Transformative Power of Surrender

The case studies of Sarah, Amir, and Linda illustrate the transformative power of surrender in various contexts—professional burnout, mental health, and personal awakening. Each individual embarked on a unique journey, yet they shared a common thread: the willingness to let go of control, embrace vulnerability, and trust in the flow of life.

Through their experiences, we learn that surrendering is not an endpoint but a continuous practice that invites us to cultivate awareness and openness. By relinquishing our attachment to outcomes, we allow life to unfold in ways we could never have imagined.

As we reflect on these stories, may we be inspired to embrace our own journeys of surrender. In doing so, we open ourselves to the richness of experience, the beauty of connection, and the transformative potential that lies within each moment. Surrendering to the flow of life invites us to dance with existence, celebrating the magic of being alive.

Chapter 8: Yogamaya in Relationships

- **The dynamics of relationships through the lens of Yogamaya**

In the realm of human experience, **relationships** serve as mirrors reflecting our innermost thoughts, desires, and fears. Yet, the dynamics of these connections can often become tangled in misunderstandings, conflicts, and illusions. Through the lens of **Yogamaya**, we come to understand that our relationships are deeply intertwined with the fabric of reality, revealing both the beautiful and complex nature of human connection. This chapter explores the dynamics of relationships through Yogamaya by delving into the intertwined lives of three individuals: **Nisha**, **Arjun**, and **Sofia**. Each character's journey reveals the transformative potential of Yogamaya in navigating the challenges and joys of human connection.

The Journey of Nisha: Seeking Authentic Connection

Nisha, a thirty-two-year-old graphic designer, had always believed in the power of love and connection. However, her relationships often left her feeling unfulfilled. Raised in a household that prioritized academic achievement and success, she struggled to express her emotions and connect deeply with others. Her upbringing instilled in her the belief that vulnerability was a weakness, leading her to create barriers around her heart.

Despite her charming personality, Nisha found herself caught in a pattern of superficial relationships, where intimacy was scarce. Her friends were often attracted to her confidence, yet they failed to see the cracks in her facade. Each failed romance deepened her sense of isolation, and she began to question whether true connection was even possible.

One evening, while attending a workshop on conscious relationships, Nisha heard a speaker discuss the concept of Yogamaya—the divine illusion that shapes our perceptions of reality. The speaker emphasized that relationships are often influenced by societal conditioning and personal beliefs, leading to the illusion of separateness. Nisha's interest was piqued; she had always sensed a disconnection between her inner world and her external relationships.

The Awakening Experience

Motivated to explore the concept further, Nisha started practicing mindfulness and self-inquiry. Each morning, she would journal her thoughts, examining the underlying beliefs that shaped her perceptions of love and connection. Through this introspective process, she began to recognize how her past experiences influenced her present relationships.

One day, as she sat in her favorite café, she watched couples interact, each person revealing their joys and sorrows through laughter and tears. In that moment, she understood the profound connection that existed between individuals—a tapestry of shared experiences woven together by love and understanding. Nisha realized that her previous fears and insecurities had blinded her to the beauty of genuine connection.

The Transformation

With newfound clarity, Nisha decided to embrace vulnerability in her relationships. She reached out to a close friend, **Sofia**, whom she had unintentionally distanced herself from due to her own fears. In a heartfelt conversation, Nisha opened up about her struggles and insecurities, allowing herself to be seen for who she truly was.

Sofia, equally moved by Nisha's honesty, reciprocated with her own story of struggle. Their conversation deepened their bond, breaking down the walls that had separated them. Nisha's willingness to embrace vulnerability and authenticity transformed her relationships, leading her to cultivate deeper connections with those around her.

The Journey of Arjun: Love and Fear

Arjun, a thirty-five-year-old entrepreneur, had always been fiercely independent. Having experienced a tumultuous childhood marked by parental separation, he developed a protective armor around his heart. Relationships felt like a threat to his autonomy, leading him to shy away from emotional intimacy.

Despite his success in business, Arjun felt an emptiness that permeated his life. He often found himself in casual relationships, convinced that commitment would lead to vulnerability and, ultimately, pain. However, a part of him yearned for a deeper connection, one that would fill the void he had long ignored.

One fateful evening, he attended a gathering where he met Nisha. Instantly drawn to her creative spirit, they exchanged numbers, but Arjun hesitated to pursue a deeper relationship. He found himself caught in the conflict between his desire for connection and his fear of losing control.

The Confrontation of Fears

After several weeks of intermittent texting and casual outings, Arjun realized that he was sabotaging his own happiness. He recalled the workshop Nisha had attended, where the concept of Yogamaya was discussed. The speaker had explained how the illusion of separation manifests in relationships, preventing individuals from experiencing the unity of existence.

Feeling inspired, Arjun reached out to Nisha and invited her for coffee. During their conversation, he shared his fears about commitment and the pain of his past. To his surprise, Nisha responded with empathy, sharing her own struggles with vulnerability.

In that moment, Arjun realized that their fears were intertwined, and their journeys were not as separate as he had once believed. The concept of Yogamaya illuminated the space between them, revealing the illusion that had held him captive. With Nisha's encouragement, Arjun began to confront his fears head-on, gradually embracing the idea that true connection could be a source of strength rather than a threat to his independence.

The Journey of Sofia: Healing Through Connection

Sofia, a compassionate healer in her forties, had spent years helping others navigate their emotional landscapes. Yet, she struggled with her own feelings of unworthiness and self-doubt. Despite her skills, she often felt disconnected from her own heart, fearing that her imperfections would drive people away.

Having observed Nisha's and Arjun's struggles, Sofia recognized a common thread in their experiences. She sensed the presence of Yogamaya in their lives—the intricate web of beliefs and conditioning that shaped their perceptions of love and connection.

The Awakening Through Reflection

One day, while meditating, Sofia was struck by a profound realization: she had been holding onto the belief that she needed to be perfect to be worthy of love. This illusion had prevented her from forming authentic connections with others. In that moment of clarity, she recognized the power of vulnerability and the healing potential of surrender.

Determined to break free from her self-imposed limitations, Sofia reached out to Nisha and Arjun. She invited them to join her in a weekly gathering focused on exploring the dynamics of relationships through the lens of Yogamaya. Together, they created a safe space to share their stories, fears, and dreams.

The Transformation of Connection

As the weeks passed, the trio forged a deep bond rooted in authenticity and mutual support. Through their discussions, they began to unravel the threads of conditioning that had shaped their relationships. They explored themes of love, fear, and the impact of societal expectations on their lives.

Sofia's gentle guidance helped Nisha and Arjun confront their insecurities, while their shared experiences provided her with the healing she had long sought. The practice of surrendering to the flow of their evolving relationships became a source of strength for each of them.

Nisha learned to trust in her ability to connect deeply with others, embracing vulnerability as a pathway to love. Arjun discovered that commitment did not equate to loss of freedom; rather, it opened the door to a more profound sense of belonging. Sofia, in turn, found healing in her connection with Nisha and Arjun, allowing her to embrace her imperfections as part of her unique journey.

The Ripple Effect: Transforming Relationships

As Nisha, Arjun, and Sofia continued to nurture their friendship, they became catalysts for change in the lives of those around them. Their willingness to embrace vulnerability and authenticity inspired others to reflect on their own relationships, encouraging a shift from superficial connections to deeper, more meaningful bonds.

Nisha began leading workshops focused on creativity and self-expression, inviting participants to explore the intersection of vulnerability and connection. Her experiences with Yogamaya resonated deeply with those seeking to navigate the complexities of relationships in a society that often celebrates independence over intimacy.

Arjun, inspired by his journey, launched a podcast where he shared candid conversations about love, fear, and the importance of connection. His willingness to share his own struggles encouraged listeners to confront their fears and seek authentic connections.

Sofia, ever the compassionate healer, organized community gatherings where individuals could explore their emotions in a safe and supportive environment. She fostered connections among participants, creating a network of support that transcended individual struggles.

Conclusion: The Unfolding of Yogamaya in Relationships

Through the intertwined journeys of Nisha, Arjun, and Sofia, we witness the transformative power of Yogamaya in shaping relationships. Their stories illuminate the intricacies of human connection, revealing how the illusion of separation can be transcended through vulnerability, empathy, and authenticity.

Yogamaya invites us to examine the beliefs and conditioning that influence our relationships, urging us to let go of the need for control and embrace the flow of life. By recognizing the divine illusion that binds us together, we can cultivate deeper connections with ourselves and others.

As we reflect on the dynamics of relationships through the lens of Yogamaya, may we be inspired to explore our own journeys of connection. Let us embrace vulnerability, celebrate our imperfections, and trust in the transformative power of love as we navigate the beautiful tapestry of human experience. In this dance of existence, we discover that we are not separate but intricately woven together in the sacred fabric of life.

- **Navigating attachments and detachment**

In the grand tapestry of human experience, **attachments** shape our relationships, aspirations, and even our identity. From childhood, we form bonds with family, friends, and environments, seeking safety, love, and validation. Yet, these attachments can also lead to pain, confusion, and suffering when they become excessive or unhealthy. In contrast, **detachment**—the practice of releasing emotional ties without losing love—offers a path toward spiritual freedom and growth. This chapter unfolds the intricate dance between attachment and detachment through the intertwined stories of three individuals: **Maya**, **Raj**, and **Elena**. Their journeys reveal the complexities of navigating attachments, the challenges of letting go, and the transformative potential of finding balance.

The Journey of Maya: The Weight of Attachment

Maya, a vibrant and ambitious woman in her late twenties, had always been a people-pleaser. Raised in a close-knit family, she learned early on that love was contingent on meeting the expectations of others. Throughout her life, she formed attachments based on the desire to be liked and accepted. While she thrived in social situations and enjoyed the company of her friends, these relationships were often marked by an unspoken pressure to conform to their needs.

In her quest for approval, Maya often neglected her own desires and aspirations. She found herself in a cycle of seeking validation from others, which left her feeling emotionally drained. Although she had a solid circle of friends, she often felt a lingering sense of emptiness.

The Catalyst for Change

One fateful evening, Maya attended a workshop on personal growth led by a charismatic speaker named **Ravi**. He spoke about the nature of attachments and how they could lead to suffering if not balanced with self-awareness and understanding. Ravi emphasized that attachments could be healthy, but when they become excessive, they could suffocate personal growth and lead to unfulfilled desires.

Intrigued, Maya listened intently as Ravi shared stories of individuals who had learned to navigate their attachments in a way that allowed them to maintain connections without losing their individuality. He encouraged participants to reflect on their attachments and consider how they might be hindering their growth.

That night, Maya returned home, her mind swirling with questions. She began journaling about her relationships, seeking clarity on the emotional bonds she had formed. As she wrote, she uncovered the truth: her desire for approval had led her to cling to people and situations that no longer served her.

The Awakening Experience

With this newfound awareness, Maya decided to explore the practice of detachment. She sought guidance from Ravi, who introduced her to mindfulness techniques that encouraged her to observe her emotions without judgment. Through meditation, Maya learned to recognize her attachment patterns, acknowledging how they influenced her choices and interactions.

Maya began implementing small changes in her daily life. She practiced saying "no" to activities that felt draining and started prioritizing her own desires and aspirations. As she learned to let go of the need for constant approval, she discovered the freedom that comes with self-acceptance.

The Transformation

Over time, Maya found herself in a state of balance. She embraced her friendships with newfound clarity, appreciating the love and support they offered without feeling obligated to meet everyone's expectations. Her relationships flourished as she learned to communicate openly about her needs, fostering deeper connections based on authenticity.

Through her journey, Maya discovered that true love does not require attachment or clinging; rather, it thrives on understanding, respect, and acceptance. As she navigated her attachments with a spirit of detachment, she began to explore new passions, from painting to hiking, reclaiming the essence of who she was beyond the roles she had previously played.

The Journey of Raj: The Fear of Letting Go

Raj, a thirty-four-year-old corporate manager, had always prided himself on his ability to maintain control in every aspect of his life. Growing up in a highly competitive environment, he had learned that success depended on hard work, discipline, and unwavering commitment. He believed that attachments were a sign of weakness; hence, he kept his relationships at arm's length.

However, beneath Raj's stoic exterior lay a deep fear of abandonment. His parents had divorced when he was young, leaving him with a belief that attachments would only lead to pain. As a result, he became a master at detaching emotionally, convincing himself that he did not need anyone. His friendships were superficial, revolving around work and leisure without delving into deeper emotional connections.

The Catalyst for Change

One day, during a team-building retreat, Raj was partnered with Maya for a group activity. As they engaged in discussions, Raj noticed Maya's openness and vulnerability, which made him uncomfortable. She shared her journey of navigating attachments, and Raj found himself intrigued, even envious of her ability to connect deeply with others.

After the retreat, Raj began to question his approach to relationships. He realized that his detachment was not a strength but rather a defense mechanism built on fear. He sought guidance from a therapist who introduced him to the concept of healthy attachments and the importance of emotional vulnerability.

The Confrontation of Fears

Through therapy, Raj learned to explore his fears surrounding attachment. He began to confront the beliefs that had shaped his relationships for years. One afternoon, while journaling, he wrote about the pain of losing his parents' relationship and how it had influenced his understanding of love.

As Raj delved deeper into his emotions, he recognized that his fear of attachment was rooted in the belief that closeness would ultimately lead to suffering. This realization marked a turning point in his journey. He began to practice mindfulness, learning to observe his thoughts and feelings without judgment.

The Transformation

Inspired by his journey, Raj decided to take small steps toward cultivating emotional connections. He reached out to old friends, reconnecting with those he had distanced himself from. In these conversations, he practiced openness, allowing himself to share his thoughts and feelings without fear of rejection.

Over time, Raj discovered the beauty of vulnerability in relationships. He learned that true strength lies not in detachment but in the courage to be authentic. His friendships deepened, and he began to find solace in the shared experiences of others. Raj's journey revealed that while attachments can be challenging, they also hold the potential for profound growth and connection.

The Journey of Elena: The Power of Detachment

Elena, a passionate yoga instructor in her early forties, had spent years exploring the balance between attachment and detachment. She had witnessed both the beauty and the challenges of relationships through her work with students. Her teachings emphasized the importance of cultivating awareness and understanding the nature of attachments.

Elena's journey was shaped by her own experiences with love and loss. After a difficult divorce, she had embarked on a spiritual path that encouraged her to let go of attachments while still embracing love. Through her practice, she learned that detachment did not equate to indifference; rather, it allowed her to love more freely without clinging to expectations.

The Awakening Experience

One day, while teaching a class on detachment, Elena shared her own story of healing. She encouraged her students to reflect on their attachments and consider how they influenced their lives. As she guided them through a meditation focused on releasing emotional ties, she felt a profound sense of connection with her students.

Elena encouraged her students to visualize their attachments as threads woven into their lives. As they inhaled, they were to acknowledge the beauty of these connections, and as they exhaled, they were to release the need to cling to them. This practice fostered a sense of freedom and acceptance in the room.

The Transformation

Through her teachings, Elena began to notice a shift within herself. As she encouraged her students to explore their own attachments, she found herself reflecting on her relationships and the balance she had cultivated. Her experience of detachment allowed her to embrace love without fear of loss. She learned that love could exist without clinging, and that true connection is not defined by possession but by acceptance.

Elena began to incorporate her teachings into her own life, embracing moments of vulnerability with friends and family. She reconnected with her ex-husband, engaging in open conversations that fostered healing and understanding. Through these interactions, she found closure and a renewed sense of love for herself and others.

Conclusion: The Dance of Attachment and Detachment

Through the journeys of Maya, Raj, and Elena, we witness the complexities of navigating attachments and detachment. Each character's story reveals the delicate balance between love and freedom, highlighting the importance of cultivating awareness in our relationships.

Attachments, when approached with mindfulness, can deepen connections and foster growth. Conversely, detachment allows for the release of unhealthy patterns and the embracing of authentic love. As we explore our own relationships, may we learn to navigate the dance of attachment and detachment with grace and understanding.

In this journey of life, let us embrace our connections while remaining open to the beauty of letting go. Through the lens of Yogamaya, we discover that love is not defined by possession but by the profound understanding that we are all interconnected in the tapestry of existence. By cultivating awareness and practicing the art of detachment, we can experience the fullness of love while honoring our individual journeys.

- **Building conscious relationships based on awareness**

In the intricate landscape of human connection, relationships serve as the mirrors reflecting our innermost thoughts, beliefs, and desires. They offer opportunities for growth, healing, and transformation. Yet, many individuals navigate their relationships unconsciously, reacting to external stimuli without a deep understanding of themselves or their partners. **Conscious relationships**, rooted in awareness, present a pathway to deeper intimacy, emotional connection, and spiritual evolution. This chapter explores the journey of three individuals—**Leela**, **Kiran**, and **Asha**—as they embark on a quest to build conscious relationships through awareness, vulnerability, and authentic communication.

The Journey of Leela: Awakening to Self-Awareness

Leela, a thirty-year-old art teacher, had always felt a longing for meaningful connections in her life. Growing up in a household where emotional expression was stifled, she often found herself in relationships marked by confusion and disappointment. Despite her vibrant personality and artistic talent, Leela struggled to articulate her feelings, leading her partners to misunderstand her intentions.

For years, she had settled for relationships that lacked depth, often choosing partners who were charming but emotionally unavailable. This pattern left her feeling unfulfilled and disconnected from her true self. One day, while attending a personal development workshop, Leela encountered the concept of **conscious relationships**. The facilitator spoke of relationships as a sacred journey of mutual growth, emphasizing the importance of self-awareness and authenticity.

The Awakening Experience

Inspired, Leela embarked on a journey of self-discovery. She began journaling her thoughts and emotions, delving into her past experiences to uncover the beliefs that shaped her relationship patterns. Through this introspective process, she identified the fear of vulnerability that had held her captive for so long.

As she explored her fears, Leela decided to confront her attachments by engaging in mindfulness practices. Each day, she dedicated time to meditation, where she learned to observe her thoughts without judgment. This practice allowed her to cultivate self-awareness and recognize the emotions that arose within her.

The Transformation

With newfound clarity, Leela began to communicate her feelings with honesty and openness. She reached out to her current partner, **Kiran**, expressing her desire for a deeper connection. During their conversations, she practiced vulnerability, sharing her fears and dreams while inviting Kiran to do the same.

Their discussions became a safe space for exploration, allowing both of them to express their needs and desires authentically. As they nurtured their connection, Leela discovered that being vulnerable did not equate to weakness; rather, it created a foundation for trust and intimacy. This transformative experience laid the groundwork for conscious relationships, where both partners embraced their individuality while honoring their bond.

The Journey of Kiran: The Art of Active Listening

Kiran, a thirty-two-year-old marketing executive, had always prided himself on being a good listener. However, he often found himself distracted, mentally rehearsing his responses while his partners spoke. This pattern of communication left him feeling disconnected, leading to misunderstandings and frustration.

When he met Leela, Kiran was immediately drawn to her artistic spirit and vibrant energy. Yet, as their relationship progressed, he sensed a growing distance. He realized that his habitual listening style was not enough to foster the intimacy he desired. Intrigued by the idea of building conscious relationships, Kiran sought guidance from Leela on how to cultivate awareness in their connection.

The Catalyst for Change

Inspired by Leela's journey, Kiran began practicing active listening—a skill he had only scratched the surface of. He committed to being fully present in their conversations, letting go of distractions and engaging with

Leela on a deeper level. He learned to ask open-ended questions that invited her to share her thoughts and feelings without interruption.

One evening, while cooking dinner together, Leela opened up about her childhood experiences and the emotional barriers she had faced. Kiran listened intently, absorbing her words while offering encouragement and support. As he embraced this new approach to communication, he noticed a shift in their dynamic—Leela felt seen, heard, and valued.

The Transformation

As Kiran continued to practice active listening, he discovered the profound impact it had on their relationship. Their conversations became richer and more meaningful, filled with laughter and vulnerability. Kiran learned to appreciate the beauty of silence, allowing space for both of them to process their emotions before responding.

In this newfound awareness, Kiran realized that conscious relationships required effort and intention. He began to cultivate mindfulness not only in his conversations with Leela but also in his daily life. By remaining present in each moment, he fostered a deeper connection to himself and his surroundings.

The Journey of Asha: Embracing Authenticity

Asha, a spirited woman in her late twenties, had spent years conforming to societal expectations. Raised in a conservative household, she had learned to suppress her true self to gain approval from her family and peers. Despite her vibrant personality, Asha often felt like a shadow of her authentic self, masking her dreams and desires.

After attending a retreat focused on conscious living, Asha became inspired to embrace authenticity in her relationships. The facilitators emphasized the importance of expressing one's true self as a pathway to building conscious connections. Asha realized that her relationships had suffered due to her reluctance to be genuine.

The Awakening Experience

Determined to shed her masks, Asha began to explore her true desires and aspirations. She engaged in creative activities, such as painting and writing, to reconnect with her authentic self. Through these practices, she discovered the joy of self-expression and began to articulate her thoughts and feelings openly.

Asha reached out to Leela and Kiran, inviting them to participate in a weekly gathering where they could explore their authentic selves. During these gatherings, the trio engaged in deep conversations, sharing their hopes, dreams, and fears. Asha's enthusiasm for authenticity inspired Leela and Kiran to deepen their commitment to conscious communication.

The Transformation

As the weeks passed, Asha's journey of authenticity transformed the dynamics of their relationships. The trio created a safe space where each individual felt empowered to share their truths without fear of judgment. Their conversations became a wellspring of inspiration and support, allowing them to grow both individually and collectively.

Asha learned that embracing her authenticity required courage, but it also fostered a profound sense of liberation. By revealing her true self to her friends, she experienced a deeper connection that transcended superficial interactions. In this journey, Asha discovered that conscious relationships flourished when individuals felt free to express their uniqueness.

The Power of Conscious Relationships

As Leela, Kiran, and Asha continued their journey toward building conscious relationships, they became a source of inspiration for those around them. Their commitment to self-awareness, active listening, and authenticity laid the groundwork for transformative connections that transcended the ordinary.

Through their experiences, they realized that conscious relationships were not merely about eliminating misunderstandings or conflicts; they were about cultivating a space for growth, love, and mutual support. Each individual became a catalyst for positive change in their community, encouraging others to explore their own relationships through the lens of awareness.

The Ripple Effect

In time, their gatherings grew, attracting more individuals who sought to cultivate conscious relationships in their lives. Each participant brought unique perspectives and stories, enriching the collective experience. They shared practices for nurturing awareness, fostering vulnerability, and embracing authenticity in their interactions.

Through workshops, discussions, and creative activities, Leela, Kiran, and Asha inspired others to embark on their own journeys of self-discovery. They emphasized that building conscious relationships required intention, practice, and a commitment to growth—both as individuals and as a community.

As they nurtured their connections, they discovered that conscious relationships were not static; they evolved with each shared experience and dialogue. Each individual became a co-creator in the tapestry of love and understanding, weaving together their unique threads of identity.

Conclusion: The Path of Conscious Relationships

Through the journeys of Leela, Kiran, and Asha, we witness the transformative power of building conscious relationships based on awareness. Their stories illuminate the importance of self-awareness, active listening, and authenticity in fostering deep connections.

As we reflect on our own relationships, may we be inspired to cultivate awareness and embrace the beauty of vulnerability. Conscious relationships offer a pathway to healing, growth, and love—a sacred journey that encourages us to honor our true selves while nurturing the bonds we share.

In this journey of life, let us strive to build conscious relationships that celebrate our individuality while fostering unity and understanding. By cultivating awareness and practicing intentional communication, we can create a tapestry of connections that enrich our lives and the lives of those around us. In this dance of existence, may we find joy in the journey of building conscious relationships, knowing that we are all interconnected in the shared experience of love and growth.

Chapter 9: The Path to Liberation (Moksha)

- **The ultimate goal: transcending illusion**

In the vast expanse of existence, the ultimate pursuit of every individual soul is the quest for **liberation**, or **Moksha**. This sacred journey seeks to transcend the illusions of the material world, ultimately leading to a profound understanding of one's true nature. Moksha represents the state of eternal bliss and freedom from the cycles of birth and death. This chapter follows the intertwined destinies of three seekers—**Arjun**, **Nisha**, and **Ravi**—as they navigate the complexities of existence, facing their illusions and striving for liberation.

The Journey of Arjun: Confronting the Illusion of Identity

Arjun, a young man in his mid-twenties, was born into a family steeped in spiritual traditions. His father, a revered guru, often spoke of the transient nature of life and the importance of seeking truth. Yet, Arjun found himself trapped in the illusion of identity. Like many, he sought validation in societal achievements: a prestigious job, a beautiful partner, and a life filled with material comforts.

Despite his outward success, Arjun felt an inner emptiness. Each accomplishment brought fleeting satisfaction, quickly overshadowed by an insatiable longing for something deeper. One evening, while attending a lecture on self-realization, he was struck by the speaker's words: "You are not your thoughts, your possessions, or your status; you are the eternal essence beyond the transient."

The Awakening Experience

These words resonated within Arjun, igniting a spark of curiosity. He began to explore the concept of **Maya**, the illusion that clouds one's true perception. Arjun immersed himself in study, reading ancient texts and engaging in discussions with spiritual teachers. He soon discovered that the layers of identity he clung to were mere constructs of the mind.

Driven by this new understanding, Arjun decided to embark on a journey of self-inquiry. He sought solitude in nature, spending time in the serene mountains where he could contemplate his existence without distractions. During his meditative practices, he confronted the beliefs that had shaped his identity. He asked himself profound questions: "Who am I beyond my name? What remains when I strip away my roles and labels?"

The Transformation

As Arjun delved deeper into his self-inquiry, he began to experience moments of clarity. In meditation, he encountered the silent observer within—an awareness that transcended his thoughts and emotions. This realization unveiled the truth that he was not the experiences he identified with but the consciousness that witnessed them.

Through these insights, Arjun learned to detach from the illusions of identity. He gradually released the need for external validation, focusing instead on cultivating an inner sense of fulfillment. With this newfound awareness, Arjun returned to his daily life, approaching relationships and work with a sense of purpose rooted in authenticity.

The Journey of Nisha: The Burden of Desire

Nisha, a spirited woman in her thirties, had spent years chasing dreams and desires that she believed would bring her happiness. Whether it was career achievements, romantic relationships, or material possessions, Nisha poured her energy into the pursuit of success. Yet, with each attainment, she found herself feeling more empty and discontented.

Her life reached a tipping point when her long-term relationship ended abruptly. The emotional turmoil left her questioning everything she had built her identity upon. Seeking solace, Nisha attended a retreat focused on spirituality and personal growth. There, she encountered a wise elder who spoke about the futility of desires and the importance of letting go.

The Catalyst for Change

In the intimate setting of the retreat, Nisha listened intently as the elder shared his own journey of relinquishing desires. "Desire is the root of suffering," he said. "When we cling to what we want, we create a gap between our present reality and our inner peace. True liberation lies in the art of surrender."

Intrigued, Nisha began to explore the concept of desire and its role in her life. She engaged in journaling, reflecting on her experiences and the underlying motivations behind her desires. Through this practice, she discovered that many of her aspirations were born from societal expectations rather than her authentic self.

The Awakening Experience

As Nisha continued her exploration, she recognized the cycle of craving and disappointment that had defined her existence. She learned about **detachment**—the ability to appreciate life's experiences without clinging to outcomes. With this understanding, Nisha started practicing mindfulness, immersing herself in the present moment and releasing her attachment to future desires.

She embraced the practice of gratitude, acknowledging the beauty of life as it was, rather than how she wished it to be. Each day, she dedicated time to meditate, focusing on her breath and cultivating awareness of her thoughts without judgment. This practice allowed her to observe her desires without being consumed by them.

The Transformation

Through her journey of self-discovery, Nisha learned that true fulfillment arises from within, not from external achievements. She began to cultivate self-love, celebrating her uniqueness and accepting herself as she was. As she let go of her desire for validation, she discovered a newfound sense of freedom.

Nisha's relationships transformed as she approached them from a place of authenticity rather than expectation. She learned to communicate openly with others, expressing her feelings without fear of rejection. This shift allowed her to form deeper connections grounded in mutual respect and understanding.

The Journey of Ravi: Embracing Surrender

Ravi, a wise and seasoned seeker in his forties, had spent decades traversing the spiritual path. He had explored various philosophies and practices, yet he felt something was still missing. Ravi's journey had led him to understand the intricacies of the material world and the illusions that clouded perception. However, he struggled with the concept of surrender, often feeling a sense of resistance when it came to relinquishing control over his life.

One evening, while meditating in his peaceful garden, Ravi encountered a profound realization: true liberation could only be achieved through **surrender**. He understood that surrendering did not equate to passivity; rather, it meant trusting the universe and embracing the flow of life.

The Awakening Experience

Inspired by this insight, Ravi began to embrace the practice of surrender in his daily life. He started by letting go of the need to control outcomes, allowing life to unfold naturally. Instead of forcing situations, he chose to flow with the currents of existence, trusting that each experience served a purpose.

During his meditation, Ravi focused on visualizing himself as a leaf floating down a gentle river. He observed how the leaf gracefully surrendered to the flow, navigating twists and turns without resistance. This image became a powerful metaphor for his journey toward liberation.

The Transformation

As Ravi embraced surrender, he experienced a profound shift in his perspective. He learned to release his attachment to specific outcomes, fostering a sense of peace in the present moment. This transformation extended to his relationships, where he began to trust his loved ones more deeply, allowing them the freedom to be themselves without judgment.

Ravi also sought to inspire others on their paths to liberation. He began leading workshops and discussions centered around surrender, encouraging participants to explore their resistance and the fear that often accompanies letting go. Through guided meditations and personal sharing, he created a safe space for individuals to confront their illusions and embrace their true selves.

The Intertwined Journeys: A Shared Vision of Liberation

As Arjun, Nisha, and Ravi each traversed their unique paths toward liberation, their journeys began to intertwine. They found themselves drawn together through a shared vision of transcending illusion and embracing authenticity.

A Gathering of Seekers

One sunny afternoon, they organized a gathering in a serene park, inviting fellow seekers to join them in exploring the themes of self-awareness, desire, and surrender. The event attracted a diverse group of individuals, each on their own journey toward liberation.

During the gathering, Arjun spoke about the importance of self-inquiry and understanding one's true nature. He shared his journey of letting go of the identities that had once defined him, inviting others to reflect on their own experiences.

Nisha followed, emphasizing the significance of surrendering desires. She shared her transformative journey, illustrating how releasing attachment had led her to a deeper connection with herself and others. Her words resonated with many, inspiring them to confront their own desires and the patterns that held them captive.

Ravi concluded the gathering by guiding a meditation focused on surrendering to the present moment. He encouraged participants to visualize themselves as leaves on a river, flowing freely and allowing the currents of life to guide them. The atmosphere was charged with a sense of peace and camaraderie as individuals embraced the collective energy of self-discovery.

The Ripple Effect of Liberation

The gathering sparked a movement among those present. Inspired by Arjun, Nisha, and Ravi, individuals began forming small groups to explore the themes of self-awareness, desire, and surrender in their lives. They engaged in discussions, shared experiences, and practiced mindfulness together, creating a supportive community dedicated to the pursuit of Moksha.

As time passed, the ripple effect of their journey spread beyond their immediate circle. More individuals joined the movement, each contributing their unique stories and insights. Together, they explored the concept of liberation through various practices: meditation, yoga, art, and dialogue.

Conclusion: The Path to Liberation

Through the intertwined journeys of Arjun, Nisha, and Ravi, we witness the profound power of transcending illusion and the quest for liberation. Their stories illuminate the importance of self-awareness, the necessity of releasing desires, and the transformative potential of surrender.

As we reflect on our own lives, may we be inspired to embark on our paths to Moksha. In the quest for liberation, let us cultivate awareness, confront our illusions, and embrace the beauty of surrender. The journey to liberation is not a solitary endeavor; it is a shared experience that invites us to connect with our true selves and one another.

In this dance of existence, may we find joy in the pursuit of liberation, knowing that each step brings us closer to our essence. As we navigate the complexities of life, may we trust the unfolding journey, recognizing that liberation is not a destination but a continuous exploration of our true nature, beyond the illusions that bind us.

- **Steps towards achieving liberation**

In the grand tapestry of existence, liberation, or **Moksha**, serves as the ultimate goal for many souls. It represents freedom from the shackles of illusion, ego, and the ceaseless cycles of birth and death. But how does one embark on this transformative journey? This chapter delves into the steps one can take toward achieving liberation through the story of **Maya**, a seeker whose life becomes a rich illustration of the path to Moksha.

Chapter 1: The Awakening of Maya

Maya, a spirited woman in her late twenties, found herself trapped in the relentless grind of modern life. Working in a high-pressure corporate job, she was constantly chasing deadlines and material success. On the surface, her life appeared fulfilling—she had a well-paying job, a stylish apartment, and a circle of friends. Yet, deep within her, a profound sense of emptiness gnawed at her soul.

One day, during a particularly exhausting week, Maya stumbled upon an ancient text while cleaning her grandmother's attic. The book, titled **"The Essence of Liberation,"** spoke of a path to Moksha that resonated deeply with her. It described liberation not as an elusive goal but as a journey through a series of steps—each one an opportunity for awakening and transformation.

Chapter 2: The First Step - Self-Inquiry

Intrigued and inspired, Maya decided to embark on the journey of self-inquiry, the first step towards liberation. She began by asking herself fundamental questions: **"Who am I beyond my roles and responsibilities?"** and **"What is the essence of my being?"**

Every morning, Maya dedicated time to sit in silence and reflect. She would jot down her thoughts in a journal, unraveling layers of her identity. What emerged was a pattern of beliefs shaped by societal conditioning—ideas about success, love, and happiness that had been imposed upon her since childhood.

Through this practice, Maya began to distinguish between her true self and the personas she had adopted. The process was enlightening, yet at times, it felt unsettling. Confronting her own beliefs challenged the very foundation upon which she had built her life. Nevertheless, she pressed on, recognizing that understanding herself was crucial for her liberation.

Chapter 3: The Second Step - Mindfulness

As Maya delved deeper into self-inquiry, she discovered the importance of **mindfulness**. This second step emphasized living in the present moment and cultivating awareness of her thoughts, feelings, and surroundings. She began to practice mindfulness meditation, setting aside time each day to observe her breath and simply be.

During her meditations, Maya encountered a flurry of thoughts—the worries about her job, her relationships, and her future. Yet, she learned to observe these thoughts without judgment, understanding that they were not her essence but transient waves in the ocean of her mind.

One particularly enlightening meditation led her to a revelation: by anchoring herself in the present moment, she could detach from the incessant chatter of her mind. This shift allowed her to appreciate the beauty of simple moments—a warm cup of tea, the laughter of friends, and the soothing rustle of leaves in the wind.

Chapter 4: The Third Step - Surrender

With the foundation of self-inquiry and mindfulness established, Maya discovered the third step toward liberation: **surrender**. This concept initially perplexed her. How could one achieve liberation by letting go? Yet, as she explored the idea further, she began to understand the profound wisdom behind it.

Maya sought guidance from a spiritual teacher, **Guru Ananda**, who spoke passionately about the art of surrender. "To surrender," he explained, "is not to relinquish control but to trust the flow of life. It is to let go of your need to force outcomes and allow the universe to guide you."

Emboldened by these teachings, Maya began to practice surrender in her daily life. She stopped worrying about her career path and instead focused on her passions. She took time off work to volunteer at a local community center, immersing herself in meaningful activities that sparked her joy. In doing so, she discovered that life began to unfold naturally, with opportunities arising in unexpected places.

Chapter 5: The Fourth Step - Letting Go of Attachments

As Maya continued her journey, she encountered the fourth step: **letting go of attachments**. She realized that many of her struggles stemmed from her attachments—whether to her job, her relationships, or even her self-image.

Maya reflected on her past relationships, particularly a toxic friendship that had drained her energy. She understood that her attachment to this person stemmed from fear of loneliness and the need for validation. In her heart, she knew that it was time to let go.

Through a process of introspection, Maya crafted a letter expressing her feelings. Instead of sending it, she read it aloud during a meditation, symbolically releasing her attachment to that relationship. This act of letting go lifted a weight off her shoulders, granting her a newfound sense of freedom.

Chapter 6: The Fifth Step - Cultivating Compassion

The next step in Maya's journey was to cultivate **compassion**—both for herself and others. She recognized that liberation was not just a personal journey but also a collective experience. The more she learned to love and accept herself, the more she could extend that love to those around her.

Maya began volunteering at a local shelter, where she interacted with individuals from diverse backgrounds, each with their own struggles and stories. These experiences deepened her understanding of human suffering and the importance of compassion in healing.

Through her work, Maya learned that true liberation was not solely about individual freedom but about creating a compassionate world where everyone could thrive. She started meditative practices focused on loving-kindness, sending positive energy to those in need, and connecting with the shared essence of humanity.

Chapter 7: The Sixth Step - Seeking Guidance

With her heart open and her mind clear, Maya recognized the significance of **seeking guidance** on the path to liberation. She began to surround herself with spiritual mentors, attending workshops and retreats that resonated with her newfound understanding.

During a transformative weekend retreat, Maya met fellow seekers who shared their journeys toward Moksha. She listened intently to their stories, realizing that each person's path was unique yet interconnected.

The experience of communal sharing brought Maya a profound sense of belonging. She learned that seeking guidance was not a sign of weakness but an acknowledgment of the interdependence of all seekers. As she engaged in discussions and explored different philosophies, her understanding of liberation deepened.

Chapter 8: The Seventh Step - Integration

The final step on Maya's journey toward liberation was **integration**. This step emphasized bringing all the insights and practices she had cultivated into her everyday life. It was about embodying the principles of self-inquiry, mindfulness, surrender, letting go, compassion, and seeking guidance in every aspect of her being.

Maya began to approach her work with a renewed perspective. She integrated mindfulness into her daily routine, taking short breaks to breathe and reconnect with herself amid the busyness. She learned to communicate openly with her colleagues, fostering an environment of collaboration and support.

In her relationships, Maya practiced compassion and understanding, embracing the imperfections of those around her. She engaged in heartfelt conversations with her friends, sharing her journey and inviting them to explore their own paths to liberation.

Conclusion: The Continuous Journey

Maya's journey toward liberation serves as a powerful reminder that achieving Moksha is not a destination but a continuous process. Each step she took brought her closer to her true essence, illuminating the path for others who seek to break free from the chains of illusion.

As she reflected on her journey, Maya understood that liberation is an evolving experience, requiring dedication, introspection, and the courage to confront one's illusions. With each step taken, she moved closer to the profound truth of her being—the realization that she is both the seeker and the sought, a spark of the divine amidst the play of existence.

In the end, the journey of liberation is an invitation for each of us to explore the depths of our own consciousness, to embrace our authentic selves, and to share our light with the world. May we all walk the path of Moksha with open hearts and curious minds, discovering the beauty of existence as we transcend the illusions that bind us.

- **The significance of community and support on the journey**

In the intricate dance of existence, each soul embarks on a journey of self-discovery, seeking liberation and understanding. While the path to **Moksha** can often feel solitary, it is profoundly enriched by the presence of **community** and **support**. This chapter explores the transformative power of togetherness through the story of **Aarav**, **Leela**, and **Samir**, three seekers who learn that the journey toward enlightenment is not just an individual pursuit but a collective endeavor.

Chapter 1: Aarav's Awakening

Aarav, a quiet and introspective man in his thirties, lived alone in a bustling city, often feeling isolated in his quest for spiritual truth. He had grown weary of the superficial connections that permeated his daily life—conversations filled with small talk and an incessant rush that left little room for genuine connection.

Aarav had recently discovered meditation and mindfulness, practices that resonated deeply with his spirit. Yet, despite the inner peace he cultivated, he felt a persistent longing for something more. He often wondered if there were others who shared his aspirations for deeper understanding and connection.

One evening, while attending a local meditation session, Aarav noticed a flyer for a spiritual community called **"The Circle of Light."** Intrigued, he decided to attend a gathering, uncertain of what to expect but eager for connection.

Chapter 2: The Circle of Light

At **The Circle of Light**, Aarav entered a cozy room filled with warmth and laughter. He was welcomed by **Leela**, a radiant woman who exuded kindness and authenticity. "Welcome! We're so glad you're here," she said, her eyes sparkling with genuine warmth.

As the gathering commenced, Aarav felt a sense of belonging wash over him. People of all ages shared their journeys, experiences, and insights into spirituality. They spoke candidly about their struggles, fears, and moments of awakening. Aarav realized that he was not alone in his quest; others had traversed similar paths, wrestling with doubt and seeking deeper meaning.

The atmosphere was charged with vulnerability and openness, creating a safe space for everyone to share their stories without judgment. For the first time in years, Aarav felt a profound connection to those around him, and it sparked a flicker of hope within his heart.

Chapter 3: Leela's Vision of Community

Leela, the guiding light of the community, believed in the power of shared experiences. She understood that spiritual journeys were often fraught with challenges and that having a supportive community could transform struggles into opportunities for growth.

Leela's vision for The Circle of Light was rooted in the belief that each member could uplift one another. She facilitated workshops on mindfulness, compassion, and self-inquiry, creating a curriculum that encouraged personal exploration while fostering collective support.

As a committed participant, Aarav engaged in discussions and group meditations, experiencing the power of collective intention. He began to understand that when individuals gather with a shared purpose, they create a potent energy that amplifies their intentions.

Chapter 4: Samir's Journey of Healing

Samir, a gentle soul in his late forties, arrived at The Circle of Light seeking healing from past traumas. For years, he had struggled with the weight of unresolved pain stemming from his childhood. The isolation of his suffering had kept him trapped in a cycle of bitterness and despair.

Through the supportive community, Samir discovered the therapeutic power of sharing his story. During a session focused on vulnerability, he opened up about his past, recounting experiences that had shaped his beliefs and behaviors. To his surprise, he found that others resonated with his struggles.

As Samir spoke, he noticed the compassionate expressions on the faces of his peers, each nodding in understanding. "You're not alone," Aarav said softly, reaching out to place a reassuring hand on Samir's shoulder. In that moment, Samir felt the barriers around his heart begin to crumble, replaced by a warmth that enveloped him.

Chapter 5: The Healing Power of Shared Experiences

The act of sharing stories became a central theme within The Circle of Light. Each member took turns revealing their vulnerabilities, creating a tapestry of resilience and strength. They explored topics such as fear, love, loss, and forgiveness—elements that bind us all as human beings.

As Samir continued to participate in the community, he learned that healing often begins in the presence of others. The process of vulnerability not only lightened his burden but also allowed him to inspire others who were grappling with their struggles. He began to see himself as a source of strength, and the healing energy he received became a wellspring from which he could give back.

Chapter 6: The Power of Accountability

In the supportive environment of The Circle of Light, accountability emerged as another crucial aspect of community. Leela encouraged members to set intentions for their spiritual growth and hold each other accountable in a loving and non-judgmental way.

Aarav found this aspect particularly enriching. With the support of his newfound friends, he set goals for his meditation practice and self-inquiry. Whenever he felt tempted to fall back into old habits, he reached out to Leela or Samir, who gently reminded him of his commitment.

The collective energy of accountability fostered a sense of responsibility within the group. Each member became a mirror for one another, reflecting the growth and progress that might have gone unnoticed if journeyed alone.

Chapter 7: Celebrating Milestones Together

As time passed, The Circle of Light became a sanctuary of celebration. They recognized and honored each other's milestones, no matter how small. Birthdays, anniversaries, and personal achievements were marked with heartfelt gatherings filled with laughter, music, and shared joy.

One particular evening, Aarav celebrated his six-month anniversary of consistent meditation practice. The community came together to honor his dedication, sharing stories of how his presence had inspired them. As they surrounded him with love and encouragement, Aarav felt a surge of gratitude—a profound realization that his journey was interwoven with the journeys of others.

Chapter 8: The Ripple Effect Beyond the Community

The significance of community extended far beyond the confines of The Circle of Light. Inspired by the love and support they cultivated, members began to engage with the wider community. They initiated service projects, held workshops for those in need, and shared their teachings with others who were seeking guidance.

The ripple effect of their collective journey became evident as more individuals joined their ranks, drawn by the energy of love and connection that radiated from the group. Together, they became a beacon of light, illuminating the path for those lost in the darkness of their struggles.

Chapter 9: The Collective Journey Towards Moksha

Aarav, Leela, and Samir continued to grow as individuals and as a community. They understood that the path to Moksha was not merely a destination but a continuous journey enriched by the bonds of love and support. They learned that liberation could be experienced in the present moment, as they embraced the beauty of connection and the depth of shared experiences.

Through their collective journey, they discovered that spiritual awakening was not solely an individual pursuit. The presence of community nurtured their growth, reminding them of the interconnectedness of all beings. In their journey toward liberation, they learned to celebrate each other's triumphs, comfort one another in times of struggle, and uplift each other as they navigated the complexities of existence.

Conclusion: The Power of Community on the Journey to Liberation

The story of Aarav, Leela, and Samir exemplifies the profound significance of community and support on the journey toward liberation. In a world often marked by isolation and disconnection, their experience underscores the importance of finding and nurturing connections with others.

Through the power of shared experiences, vulnerability, accountability, and celebration, community becomes a sanctuary for growth and healing. It is within this sacred space that individuals can explore their true selves, confront their fears, and embrace their journeys toward Moksha.

As we reflect on our own lives, let us remember the importance of community in our quest for liberation. May we seek out and cultivate supportive relationships that nurture our growth, inspire our journeys, and illuminate the path to our true essence. In the embrace of community, we can transcend the illusions of separateness and discover the beauty of togetherness, forging a collective journey toward the ultimate realization of our interconnectedness in the tapestry of existence.

Conclusion

- Recap of the key themes

As we draw the curtain on this journey through the intricate layers of reality, the path of Yogamaya, and the quest for liberation, it becomes essential to reflect on the key themes that have emerged throughout our exploration. This conclusion seeks not only to recap these themes but also to weave them into a tapestry that illustrates the profound interconnectedness of existence.

The Duality of Reality: Maya and Yogamaya

At the heart of our journey lies the duality of reality—the interplay between **Maya** and **Yogamaya**. Maya, often understood as the illusion of the material world, challenges us to see beyond the surface and confront the layers of belief and conditioning that shape our perceptions. It is the veil that clouds our true understanding of existence, leading us to identify with transient experiences, attachments, and ego-driven pursuits.

Conversely, Yogamaya embodies the divine play of creation, a force that both conceals and reveals the ultimate truth. It invites us to embrace the interplay of light and shadow, encouraging us to delve into the depths of our consciousness and discover the essence of who we truly are. This duality serves as a reminder that liberation is not about rejecting the material world but rather understanding it as a vital aspect of our spiritual evolution.

The Role of Divine Play (Lila)

The concept of **Lila**—divine play—permeates the narratives we explored, illustrating that the universe unfolds through a creative dance of joy and spontaneity. Lila teaches us that existence is not a rigid structure but a fluid expression of life's myriad possibilities. Through the lens of Lila, we come to understand that our struggles and challenges are part of a grand design, contributing to the richness of our experiences.

This playful aspect of existence encourages us to adopt a sense of lightness as we navigate life's complexities. By recognizing that we are participants in a divine play, we cultivate resilience and adaptability, allowing us to embrace life's uncertainties with open hearts.

The Journey of Awakening and Liberation

As we traversed the path of **spiritual awakening**, we encountered the signs that illuminate our journey—moments of clarity, heightened awareness, and profound connections with ourselves and others. The techniques for recognizing and transcending illusion became vital tools in our quest for liberation, empowering us to dismantle the barriers that separate us from our true essence.

The significance of **self-inquiry and mindfulness** emerged as a powerful practice for awakening our consciousness. Through these techniques, we cultivated a deeper understanding of our thoughts and emotions, paving the way for authentic self-expression and connection with the divine.

The Importance of Surrender and Grace

In our exploration of **divine grace** and the importance of surrendering to the flow of life, we discovered the transformative power of letting go. Surrender is not an act of defeat but a profound acceptance of the present moment. It invites us to trust in the unfolding of our lives, recognizing that every experience is an opportunity for growth.

The stories of transformation through surrender illustrated how grace can manifest in unexpected ways. By surrendering to the divine flow, we open ourselves to possibilities that transcend our limited understanding, leading us to a deeper connection with our purpose and the universe.

Relationships as Mirrors of Growth

As we examined the dynamics of relationships through the lens of **Yogamaya**, we learned that connections with others serve as mirrors reflecting our inner world. The journey of navigating attachments and detachment became a vital theme, emphasizing the importance of building conscious relationships based on awareness and compassion.

In recognizing that relationships are opportunities for growth and healing, we cultivated the ability to connect authentically with others. This journey taught us that liberation is intertwined with our capacity to love and support one another, fostering a sense of community and belonging.

The Role of Community and Collective Support

The significance of **community** and support resonated deeply throughout our exploration. The experiences of Aarav, Leela, and Samir underscored the power of shared journeys and the healing that arises from vulnerability. Community provides a sanctuary where we can express our struggles, celebrate our triumphs, and uplift one another on the path to liberation.

In an increasingly disconnected world, the importance of finding and nurturing connections cannot be overstated. Together, we create a tapestry of support that enriches our spiritual journeys, reminding us that we are never alone in our quest for understanding and enlightenment.

The Continuous Journey Towards Moksha

Ultimately, our exploration culminated in the understanding that **Moksha**—liberation—is not a fixed destination but a continuous journey. It invites us to embrace the present moment, recognizing that each step we take brings us closer to our true essence. The path to Moksha is marked by dedication, introspection, and the courage to confront the illusions that bind us.

As we navigate the complexities of existence, we are called to celebrate the journey itself, trusting in the unfolding of our lives. The themes we have explored serve as guiding lights, illuminating the path to self-discovery, connection, and liberation.

Final Reflections: Embracing the Journey

In conclusion, the journey through the layers of reality, the divine play of existence, and the quest for liberation reveals the beauty and complexity of our human experience. Each theme we have woven together contributes to a larger understanding of ourselves and the universe we inhabit.

As we continue to walk our unique paths, may we carry these insights with us—embracing the duality of life, celebrating the power of community, and surrendering to the divine flow. In doing so, we honor the sacred dance of existence, recognizing that we are all interconnected threads in the tapestry of life, forever intertwined in the pursuit of truth and liberation.

Epilogue: The Call to Action

As we conclude this exploration, I invite you, dear reader, to reflect on your own journey. Consider the themes that resonate with you and the steps you can take toward greater awareness, connection, and liberation. Embrace the beauty of your unique path, knowing that you are an integral part of the grand tapestry of existence.

Let us step into the world with open hearts, ready to engage with the divine play of life, fostering connections that uplift and inspire. In this journey, may we find joy, purpose, and a profound sense of belonging as we continue to seek the essence of who we are, transcending the illusions that bind us and illuminating the way for others on the path to liberation.

- **Encouragement for continued exploration of Yogamaya**

As we conclude our journey through the profound realms of Yogamaya and the interconnected tapestry of existence, it is essential to embrace the invitation for continued exploration. The path of spiritual growth is not linear; it is a dynamic journey filled with discoveries, challenges, and moments of awakening. In this final section, I encourage you to delve deeper into the teachings of Yogamaya, inviting its wisdom into your life.

Embrace Curiosity

Curiosity is a powerful catalyst for exploration. As you navigate the complexities of life, allow yourself to ask questions that arise from your heart and mind. What does Yogamaya mean to you personally? How does it manifest in your experiences? Approach these inquiries with an open heart and a willingness to learn. Each question holds the potential to unveil layers of understanding that contribute to your spiritual evolution.

Cultivate Awareness

Awareness is a cornerstone of Yogamaya. As you continue your journey, practice cultivating a heightened sense of awareness in your daily life. Pay attention to your thoughts, emotions, and reactions. Notice the moments when you feel connected to the divine play of existence and the times when you may feel lost in illusion. This awareness will serve as a guiding light, helping you navigate the intricate dance between Maya and Yogamaya.

Engage in Self-Inquiry

Self-inquiry is a transformative practice that invites you to explore the depths of your being. Set aside time for introspection, journaling, or contemplative meditation. Ask yourself, "What illusions am I holding onto? What truths do I seek?" Allow your inner voice to guide you toward deeper understanding. Self-inquiry fosters a sense of clarity and enables you to recognize the patterns that shape your reality, paving the way for liberation.

Connect with Nature

Nature is a profound teacher that embodies the principles of Yogamaya. Spend time in natural surroundings, allowing the beauty and tranquility of the environment to nourish your spirit. Observe the cycles of life, the ebb and flow of seasons, and the interconnectedness of all living beings. Nature serves as a reminder of the divine play unfolding around you, inviting you to embrace your place within it.

Foster Community and Connection

As highlighted throughout our exploration, community is a vital aspect of the journey toward understanding Yogamaya. Seek out like-minded individuals who share your interests and aspirations. Engage in discussions, attend workshops, or participate in spiritual gatherings. By connecting with others, you will find support, inspiration, and opportunities for shared growth.

Consider forming or joining a group dedicated to exploring the themes of Yogamaya. Together, you can share insights, discuss challenges, and celebrate breakthroughs. The collective energy of a supportive community amplifies individual journeys, creating a rich environment for exploration and healing.

Practice Mindfulness and Meditation

Integrating mindfulness and meditation into your daily routine is essential for deepening your connection with Yogamaya. Dedicate time each day to sit in stillness, allowing thoughts to arise and dissolve. Practice mindfulness in your everyday activities—whether eating, walking, or simply breathing. By anchoring yourself in the present moment, you cultivate a deeper awareness of the interplay between the material and spiritual realms.

Embrace the Dance of Life

Yogamaya invites us to participate in the divine dance of existence. Embrace the spontaneity of life and allow yourself to experience the joy, laughter, and playfulness inherent in being human. When challenges arise, view them as opportunities for growth rather than obstacles. Embrace the flow of life, trusting that each experience contributes to your spiritual evolution.

Conclusion: Your Unique Journey Awaits

As you embark on this ongoing exploration of Yogamaya, remember that your journey is unique and deeply personal. There is no destination to reach, only experiences to embrace and lessons to learn. Honor the ebb and flow of your path, recognizing that each step taken in curiosity, awareness, and connection brings you closer to the truth of your being.

In the words of the ancient sages, "The journey is the destination." Allow yourself to revel in the unfolding of your life, knowing that the teachings of Yogamaya are ever-present, waiting to guide you toward deeper understanding, connection, and liberation. As you continue this exploration, may you discover the beauty of existence, the joy of being fully present, and the profound interconnectedness that binds us all.

Embrace the adventure ahead, dear seeker, and let the light of Yogamaya illuminate your path as you dance through the sacred play of life.

- **Final thoughts on living beyond illusion**

As we draw our exploration to a close, it is vital to reflect on the profound implications of living beyond illusion—a theme that resonates deeply within the teachings of Yogamaya and the path to spiritual awakening. In this final chapter, we will journey through the essence of transcending the illusions that bind us and explore what it means to live a life grounded in truth, authenticity, and divine connection.

The Nature of Illusion

Illusion is an intrinsic part of the human experience, often rooted in our perceptions, beliefs, and conditioning. Maya, the grand illusion, envelops us in a web of distractions, attachments, and desires, leading us to identify with the transient and the superficial. We become entangled in the narratives of our minds, often mistaking them for reality. This identification fosters a sense of separation—from ourselves, from others, and from the divine source that connects us all.

Living within this illusion can lead to a sense of discontent, a feeling of being lost or unfulfilled. We chase after external validations, seeking happiness in material possessions, achievements, or societal approval. Yet, the momentary pleasures these pursuits provide often dissolve, leaving us yearning for something deeper—something that resonates with the core of our being.

The Awakening to Truth

The journey of awakening begins with the realization that we are more than the roles we play or the identities we adopt. It invites us to delve beneath the layers of illusion and uncover the truth that lies within. This truth is not merely an intellectual understanding but a profound experience that transforms our perception of reality.

When we awaken to the truth of our existence, we recognize that we are interconnected beings, woven into the fabric of the universe. We are not separate from each other or from the divine; we are expressions of the same source, manifesting in unique ways. This realization shifts our focus from individualistic pursuits to a more expansive understanding of our place in the cosmic dance.

Embracing Authenticity

Living beyond illusion calls for authenticity—a commitment to being true to ourselves, to our values, and to our essence. It requires us to peel away the masks we wear and to embrace vulnerability. In a world that often prioritizes conformity, authenticity can feel like a radical act.

Embracing authenticity allows us to live in alignment with our inner truth, cultivating relationships rooted in honesty and compassion. We learn to express ourselves freely, to share our stories, and to connect deeply with others. This authenticity fosters an environment of trust and understanding, where we can support one another in our journeys of growth and healing.

The Role of Mindfulness

Mindfulness emerges as a vital practice in the quest to live beyond illusion. It invites us to be fully present in each moment, to observe our thoughts, emotions, and sensations without judgment. Through mindfulness, we develop the capacity to discern between the transient nature of our thoughts and the deeper, more enduring aspects of our being.

In moments of mindfulness, we become aware of the patterns that perpetuate our illusions. We recognize the stories we tell ourselves, the fears that hold us back, and the attachments that bind us. With this awareness, we gain the ability to respond to life from a place of clarity rather than reactivity, choosing actions that align with our true essence.

The Power of Surrender

To live beyond illusion is to embrace the power of surrender. Surrendering does not imply passivity or resignation; rather, it is an active engagement with the flow of life. It is the recognition that we are part of a greater tapestry, and our individual journeys contribute to the unfolding of the whole.

In surrendering to the divine flow, we relinquish our need for control and certainty. We learn to trust that life is unfolding as it should, even when faced with challenges or uncertainties. This surrender opens us to the possibility of grace—an effortless support that guides us toward our highest potential.

Cultivating Compassion and Love

As we awaken to the truth of our interconnectedness, we naturally cultivate compassion and love for ourselves and others. Living beyond illusion invites us to let go of judgments, grudges, and resentments that arise from a sense of separation. Instead, we recognize the shared human experience of suffering and joy.

Compassion allows us to connect with others on a deeper level, fostering an environment of empathy and understanding. It reminds us that we are all navigating our own journeys, each facing unique challenges and victories. In cultivating love, we contribute to a ripple effect of healing in the world, empowering others to awaken to their own truths.

The Ongoing Journey of Exploration

Living beyond illusion is not a destination; it is an ongoing journey of exploration and growth. Each moment presents an opportunity to deepen our understanding, to confront our illusions, and to align more closely with our true selves. As we navigate this journey, we may encounter moments of doubt, fear, and confusion. Yet, these moments are not setbacks but integral parts of the process.

In embracing the fluidity of this journey, we cultivate resilience and adaptability. We learn to embrace the uncertainty of life with grace, recognizing that our true power lies in our ability to respond with love, awareness, and authenticity.

Conclusion: A Call to Live Beyond Illusion

In closing, I invite you to reflect on your own journey of living beyond illusion. What illusions have you encountered in your life? How can you deepen your commitment to authenticity, mindfulness, and compassion? Consider the ways in which you can embrace the divine play of existence, trusting in the unfolding of your unique path.

As you step forward into the world, carry with you the insights gained from this exploration. Embrace the dance of life, knowing that each moment holds the potential for awakening and transformation. Trust in your ability to navigate the complexities of existence, and allow the light of truth to illuminate your path.

In this beautiful journey of life, may you find the courage to transcend illusion, the wisdom to embrace authenticity, and the love to connect deeply with yourself and others. Together, let us celebrate the sacred dance of existence, living fully in the truth of who we are and the profound interconnectedness that binds us all.

Appendix

• **Recommended readings and resources**

As you continue on your journey to explore the profound concepts of Yogamaya, illusion, and spiritual awakening, the following appendix serves as a curated list of recommended readings and resources. Each entry is designed to deepen your understanding, inspire your practice, and connect you with the wisdom of various traditions and teachings. This journey is both individual and collective, and these resources will help guide you along the way.

Foundational Texts

1. **The Bhagavad Gita**

    o *Author: Anonymous*

    o This timeless scripture offers profound insights into the nature of reality, the self, and the path to liberation. Through the dialogue between Arjuna and Krishna, readers are introduced to the concepts of duty (dharma), devotion (bhakti), and the nature of the soul (atman). The Gita serves as a foundational text for understanding Yogic philosophy and the interplay between the material and spiritual realms.

2. **The Upanishads**

    o *Author: Anonymous*

    o Considered the philosophical culmination of the Vedas, the Upanishads explore the nature of existence, consciousness, and the ultimate reality (Brahman). These ancient texts delve into the concepts of Maya and the quest for knowledge, encouraging readers to seek the truth that lies beyond the illusion of the material world.

3. **The Yoga Sutras of Patanjali**

    o *Author: Patanjali*

    o This classic text on Yoga philosophy outlines the eightfold path (Ashtanga Yoga) and provides practical guidance for achieving spiritual awakening. The Yoga Sutras emphasize the importance of meditation, self-discipline, and ethical living as essential tools for transcending illusion and realizing one's true nature.

Contemporary Insights

4. **The Power of Now: A Guide to Spiritual Enlightenment**

- Author: Eckhart Tolle
- Tolle's bestselling book explores the significance of present-moment awareness and the nature of the ego. Through practical exercises and insights, Tolle encourages readers to transcend the limitations of thought and connect with their true essence. This book serves as a modern companion to ancient wisdom, offering practical tools for awakening.

5. **A New Earth: Awakening to Your Life's Purpose**

    - Author: Eckhart Tolle
    - In this follow-up to *The Power of Now*, Tolle delves deeper into the collective ego and the role of consciousness in personal and societal transformation. He provides insights on living authentically and embracing the present moment, making it an essential read for those seeking to navigate the complexities of modern existence.

6. **The Untethered Soul: The Journey Beyond Yourself**

    - Author: Michael A. Singer
    - Singer's work explores the nature of consciousness and the concept of the inner voice. He invites readers to observe their thoughts and emotions without attachment, guiding them toward a deeper understanding of their true selves. This book offers practical techniques for freeing oneself from the confines of the mind, ultimately leading to liberation.

Spiritual Practices

7. **The Miracle of Mindfulness: An Introduction to the Practice of Meditation**

    - Author: Thich Nhat Hanh
    - This foundational text on mindfulness introduces readers to the practice of meditation and the importance of being present. Thich Nhat Hanh's gentle guidance encourages a deep connection with the present moment, fostering awareness and compassion. This book serves as a practical guide to incorporating mindfulness into daily life.

8. **Radical Acceptance: Embracing Your Life with the Heart of a Buddha**

    - Author: Tara Brach
    - Brach's work focuses on the concept of self-acceptance as a means of overcoming suffering and cultivating compassion. Through stories, guided meditations, and practical exercises, she invites readers to embrace their full humanity, fostering healing and awakening in the process.

9. **The Heart of the Buddha's Teaching: Transforming Suffering into Peace, Joy, and Liberation**

    - Author: Thich Nhat Hanh

- In this comprehensive guide, Thich Nhat Hanh presents the core teachings of Buddhism, including the Four Noble Truths and the Eightfold Path. He provides practical insights on transforming suffering and cultivating mindfulness, making it a valuable resource for anyone seeking a deeper understanding of spiritual practices.

Exploring Yogamaya and the Nature of Reality

10. **I Am That: Talks with Sri Nisargadatta Maharaj**
    - *Author: Sri Nisargadatta Maharaj*
    - This collection of dialogues with the Indian sage presents profound teachings on non-duality and the nature of the self. Nisargadatta's direct and unembellished approach invites readers to question their beliefs about identity and reality, offering insights into the nature of existence and consciousness.

11. **The Divine Play: The Mystical Teachings of Sri Ramakrishna**
    - *Author: Swami Vivekananda*
    - In this exploration of the life and teachings of Sri Ramakrishna, Vivekananda captures the essence of divine play (Lila) and the interconnectedness of all paths to truth. This book inspires readers to embrace the richness of spiritual experiences and recognize the beauty in diverse expressions of faith.

Online Resources and Courses

12. **Insight Timer**
    - *Website: Insight Timer*
    - This popular meditation app offers a vast library of guided meditations, courses, and talks by experienced teachers from various traditions. It provides a supportive community for individuals seeking to deepen their meditation practice and connect with others on a similar journey.

13. **The Shift Network**
    - *Website: The Shift Network*
    - The Shift Network offers a variety of online courses, summits, and events focused on personal transformation, spiritual growth, and holistic living. With offerings from renowned teachers and thought leaders, this platform provides resources for individuals seeking to explore diverse spiritual practices.

14. **Sounds True**
    - *Website: Sounds True*
    - Sounds True is a publisher of books, courses, and audio programs on spirituality, mindfulness, and personal growth. Their extensive catalog includes teachings from

prominent spiritual teachers and offers resources for those seeking to deepen their understanding of Yogamaya and related themes.

Final Thoughts on Exploration

The journey of exploring Yogamaya, living beyond illusion, and seeking spiritual awakening is a lifelong endeavor. The recommended readings and resources provided here are mere stepping stones on this path, each offering unique insights and perspectives to enrich your understanding.

As you delve into these texts and resources, approach them with an open heart and a sense of curiosity. Allow the teachings to resonate with your own experiences, integrating the wisdom into your daily life. Remember that the journey is as important as the destination, and every exploration brings you closer to understanding the profound interconnectedness of existence.

Whether through ancient scriptures, contemporary insights, or experiential practices, may you find the guidance and inspiration you seek. Embrace the divine play of life, trusting in the unfolding of your journey as you continue to explore the depths of Yogamaya and the limitless possibilities of your existence.

- **Guided meditations and exercises**

Embarking on a journey of self-discovery and spiritual awakening requires not only knowledge but also practical tools that allow us to experience and integrate the teachings of Yogamaya into our lives. Guided meditations and exercises serve as invaluable resources on this path, providing a direct experience of the concepts we have explored. This chapter is dedicated to a series of guided meditations and exercises designed to deepen your connection with Yogamaya, enhance your mindfulness practice, and support your spiritual evolution.

The Power of Guided Meditation

Meditation is a powerful tool for exploring the depths of consciousness and transcending the limitations of the mind. Through guided meditation, a facilitator offers instructions and prompts that help participants focus their attention and engage in a specific practice. This can be particularly beneficial for those who are new to meditation or those seeking to deepen their practice.

Benefits of Guided Meditation:

- **Focus and Clarity:** Guided meditation provides a framework for directing attention, helping to quiet the mind and reduce distractions.

- **Support and Comfort:** Listening to a soothing voice can create a sense of safety and relaxation, allowing participants to surrender to the experience.

- **Structure for Exploration:** Guided meditations can lead practitioners through specific themes, such as self-discovery, healing, or connecting with higher consciousness.

Preparation for Meditation

Before diving into the guided meditations and exercises, it is essential to prepare the mind and body to create an optimal environment for the practice. Here are some steps to help you prepare:

1. **Create a Sacred Space:** Choose a quiet and comfortable space where you can sit or lie down without distractions. Consider adding elements that inspire tranquility, such as candles, crystals, or incense.

2. **Set an Intention:** Take a moment to reflect on your intentions for the meditation. What do you wish to explore or experience? Setting a clear intention can enhance the depth of your practice.

3. **Ground Yourself:** Take a few deep breaths, inhaling through your nose and exhaling through your mouth. Allow your breath to become natural, focusing on the sensation of the air entering and leaving your body. Feel your connection to the earth beneath you, grounding you in the present moment.

Guided Meditation: Connecting with Yogamaya

Duration: 20-30 minutes
Objective: To cultivate awareness of the interplay between illusion and reality, allowing for a deeper connection with Yogamaya.

1. **Begin with Breath Awareness:** Close your eyes and take a few deep breaths. Inhale deeply, filling your lungs with air, and exhale slowly, releasing any tension. With each breath, allow yourself to sink deeper into relaxation.

2. **Visualize a Golden Light:** Imagine a warm, golden light surrounding you. With each breath, feel this light expanding, enveloping your entire being. This light represents the essence of Yogamaya—the divine play that permeates existence.

3. **Reflect on Illusion and Reality:** As you bask in this golden light, contemplate the nature of reality and illusion. Notice the thoughts that arise. Are there beliefs or patterns that contribute to feelings of separation or limitation? Acknowledge these thoughts without judgment and gently let them drift away like clouds in the sky.

4. **Connect with Your True Essence:** With each breath, invite the golden light to penetrate deeper into your being, illuminating the core of who you are. Visualize this light merging with your heart center, radiating warmth and love. Feel the presence of your true essence—the part of you that is unchanging and eternally connected to the universe.

5. **Embrace Stillness:** Allow yourself to simply be in this space of light and awareness. Embrace the stillness, knowing that you are part of the greater tapestry of life. When thoughts arise, gently return your focus to the sensation of the golden light.

6. **Gradually Return:** When you feel ready, slowly bring your awareness back to the present moment. Wiggle your fingers and toes, take a deep breath, and when you're ready, open your eyes. Take a moment to reflect on your experience, allowing insights to surface.

Exercise: Journaling for Self-Inquiry

Objective: To engage in self-inquiry and reflection, allowing for deeper understanding and integration of the teachings of Yogamaya.

1. **Set the Scene:** Find a quiet space with your journal and pen. Take a few deep breaths, grounding yourself in the present moment.

2. **Reflect on Your Illusions:** Begin by writing down any beliefs, fears, or patterns that you feel may be contributing to your sense of separation or limitation. Consider questions such as:
    - What stories do I tell myself that keep me stuck?
    - Are there attachments that I find difficult to let go of?
    - How do these beliefs shape my perception of reality?

3. **Explore Your True Essence:** After reflecting on your illusions, shift your focus to your true essence. Write about the qualities that define your authentic self. Consider questions like:
    - What brings me joy and fulfillment?
    - In moments of stillness, what do I feel is my true nature?
    - How can I embrace my authentic self more fully in my daily life?

4. **Set Intentions for Growth:** Conclude your journaling session by writing down three intentions for your spiritual growth. These intentions should be specific and actionable, guiding you toward greater awareness and authenticity.

5. **Review Regularly:** Revisit your journal entries regularly to track your progress and reflect on any shifts in your perspective or understanding.

Guided Meditation: Surrendering to the Flow of Life

Duration: 15-25 minutes
Objective: To cultivate a sense of surrender and trust in the unfolding of life, embracing the divine play of Yogamaya.

1. **Begin with Breath Awareness:** Find a comfortable seated position. Close your eyes and take a few deep breaths. With each inhalation, invite a sense of calm, and with each exhalation, release tension.

2. **Visualize a River:** Picture yourself sitting by a gentle river, watching the water flow effortlessly. Imagine the river representing the flow of life—the divine current that carries you forward.

3. **Surrender to the Flow:** As you sit by the river, imagine surrendering any burdens, worries, or fears into the flowing water. Visualize these feelings dissolving as they are carried away downstream. Allow yourself to feel lighter and more at peace with each breath.

4. **Affirm Your Trust:** In this space of surrender, repeat to yourself: "I trust the flow of life. I surrender to the divine play of existence." Feel the resonance of these affirmations as they sink into your being.

5. **Connect with the Present Moment:** Allow yourself to simply be in this moment, embracing the stillness and the flow around you. Trust that you are exactly where you need to be in your journey.

6. **Gradually Return:** When you feel ready, gently bring your awareness back to the room. Wiggle your fingers and toes, take a deep breath, and open your eyes. Take a moment to reflect on your experience and the feelings of surrender that arose.

Conclusion: Integrating Meditation and Exercises into Daily Life

The guided meditations and exercises presented in this chapter are designed to support you on your journey of self-discovery and spiritual awakening. As you explore the teachings of Yogamaya, remember that integration is key. The insights gained from these practices can be woven into your daily life, creating a tapestry of awareness, authenticity, and connection.

Incorporate Daily Practice:

- Set aside dedicated time for meditation and self-inquiry each day, even if it's just for a few minutes.
- Reflect on your experiences in a journal to deepen your understanding.
- Share your insights with a supportive community or trusted friends, fostering connections that enrich your journey.

By embracing these practices, you cultivate a deeper relationship with yourself and the world around you. You will find that the teachings of Yogamaya become not just concepts to ponder but lived experiences that transform your reality. Through guided meditations and reflective exercises, you can navigate the illusions of life with grace, authenticity, and love, moving ever closer to the truth of your being.

- **Glossary of terms related to Yogamaya and Hindu philosophy**

As we journey through the intricate landscape of Yogamaya and Hindu philosophy, understanding the terminology associated with these concepts is crucial. Each term carries profound significance and encapsulates the essence of ancient wisdom. This glossary serves as a guide to help readers navigate the rich tapestry of ideas presented in this exploration. Each entry is not just a definition but an invitation to delve deeper into the interconnectedness of these teachings.

A

Advaita
Advaita is a Sanskrit term meaning "non-duality." It is a philosophical concept that posits the oneness of the individual soul (Atman) and the universal consciousness (Brahman). In Advaita Vedanta, practitioners seek to realize their true nature as not separate from the divine, emphasizing the illusion of duality created by Maya. This perspective encourages individuals to transcend the apparent distinctions between self and other, recognizing the interconnectedness of all existence.

Atman
Atman refers to the individual self or soul in Hindu philosophy. It is considered the eternal, unchanging essence of a person, often equated with Brahman, the ultimate reality. The realization of Atman is central to spiritual awakening, as it involves recognizing one's true identity beyond the physical body and the ego. Understanding Atman leads to liberation (Moksha) from the cycles of birth and death (Samsara).

B

Bhakti
Bhakti translates to "devotion" and is a key aspect of Hindu spirituality. It emphasizes love and devotion to a personal deity, often characterized by surrender, trust, and emotional connection. The practice of Bhakti encourages devotees to cultivate a personal relationship with the divine, fostering a sense of unity and belonging. This path is accessible to all, regardless of background or knowledge, making it a popular and inclusive approach to spirituality.

Brahman
Brahman is the ultimate, unchanging reality in Hindu philosophy. It is often described as the source of all existence, the universal consciousness that pervades everything. Brahman transcends form and attributes, embodying both immanence and transcendence. Realizing Brahman involves understanding the nature of reality beyond the illusions created by Maya, leading to spiritual liberation.

D

Dharma
Dharma refers to the moral and ethical duties, responsibilities, and laws that govern an individual's life. In Hindu philosophy, it is the path of righteousness and living in accordance with cosmic order. Dharma varies according to one's age, caste, gender, and situation, emphasizing the importance of context in ethical decision-making. Following one's Dharma leads to harmony in personal and social life, contributing to spiritual growth and fulfillment.

I

Illusion (Maya)
Maya is the concept of illusion in Hindu philosophy, representing the deceptive nature of the material world. It refers to the veil that obscures the true nature of reality, creating the perception of separateness and duality. Maya can manifest in various forms, such as attachment, desire, and ignorance. Recognizing and transcending Maya is essential for spiritual awakening, allowing individuals to see beyond the surface and connect with the deeper truths of existence.

K

Karma
Karma translates to "action" and refers to the principle of cause and effect that governs the universe. Every action, whether physical, verbal, or mental, creates an imprint on the individual's consciousness, influencing future experiences. Positive actions generate good karma, leading to beneficial outcomes, while negative actions result in adverse consequences. Understanding karma encourages individuals to live mindfully, recognizing the interconnectedness of all actions and their impact on oneself and others.

L

Lila
Lila, often translated as "divine play," refers to the cosmic playfulness of the divine. It describes the creative and playful aspect of God, emphasizing that existence is an expression of this playful energy. Lila suggests that the universe is not merely a mechanical system but a dynamic and vibrant expression of consciousness. Recognizing life as Lila encourages individuals to embrace the fluidity of existence, finding joy and meaning in the unfolding of experiences.

M

Moksha
Moksha refers to spiritual liberation or enlightenment—the ultimate goal of human existence in Hindu philosophy. It signifies freedom from the cycles of birth, death, and rebirth (Samsara), achieved through self-realization and the understanding of one's true nature. Moksha represents the end of suffering and the realization of oneness with the divine, leading to eternal peace and bliss.

Mantra
A mantra is a sacred sound, word, or phrase that is repeated during meditation or prayer. It serves as a tool for focusing the mind, invoking specific energies, and connecting with higher consciousness. Mantras can be simple syllables, like "Om," or more complex phrases, often derived from ancient scriptures. The repetition of mantras is believed to elevate consciousness, facilitating spiritual growth and transformation.

N

Nirvana
Nirvana is a term often associated with Buddhism, representing the state of liberation from suffering and the cycles of rebirth. In Hindu philosophy, it aligns closely with the concept of Moksha. Nirvana signifies the extinguishing of desires and attachments, leading to the realization of ultimate truth and unity with the divine. It is a state of profound peace, beyond the dualities of existence.

R

Raja Yoga
Raja Yoga, often referred to as the "royal path," is one of the four main paths of yoga outlined in Hindu philosophy. It emphasizes the practice of meditation and the control of the mind as a means to attain self-realization and spiritual awakening. Raja Yoga incorporates techniques such as breath control (Pranayama), concentration (Dharana), and meditation (Dhyana) to achieve inner peace and union with the divine.

S

Samsara
Samsara refers to the continuous cycle of birth, death, and rebirth in Hindu philosophy. It embodies the journey of the soul through various lifetimes, shaped by the karma accumulated from past actions. Samsara is often viewed as a state of suffering, driven by attachment and desire. The ultimate goal of spiritual practice is to transcend Samsara and attain Moksha, liberating the soul from the cycle of rebirth.

Sadhana
Sadhana is a Sanskrit term meaning "spiritual practice." It encompasses various disciplines, techniques, and rituals undertaken by individuals to achieve spiritual goals. Sadhana may include meditation, yoga, chanting, or devotion, tailored to an individual's path and inclinations. Consistent practice fosters growth, self-awareness, and connection to the divine, ultimately leading to spiritual awakening.

Sankhya
Sankhya is a dualistic philosophical system that forms the basis of several schools of Hindu thought. It distinguishes between Purusha (consciousness) and Prakriti (matter), emphasizing the interplay between

the two. Sankhya philosophy provides insights into the nature of reality and the human experience, offering a framework for understanding the path to liberation.

T

Tamas, Rajas, and Sattva
These three Gunas (qualities) represent the fundamental energies that shape human behavior and consciousness. Tamas embodies inertia and darkness, Rajas signifies activity and passion, and Sattva represents purity and harmony. Understanding the interplay of these qualities is essential for self-awareness and spiritual growth, as individuals seek to cultivate Sattva while transcending the influences of Tamas and Rajas.

V

Vedas
The Vedas are the oldest sacred texts of Hinduism, composed in ancient Sanskrit. They consist of four primary collections: Rigveda, Samaveda, Yajurveda, and Atharvaveda. The Vedas encompass hymns, rituals, philosophy, and knowledge, forming the foundation of Hindu spirituality and philosophy. They provide insights into the nature of the universe, the self, and the divine, influencing countless generations of seekers.

Vedanta
Vedanta is a philosophical system that focuses on the teachings of the Upanishads and the nature of reality. It explores the relationship between Atman and Brahman, emphasizing the path to self-realization and liberation. Vedanta encompasses various sub-schools, including Advaita (non-dualism) and Dvaita (dualism), each offering unique perspectives on the ultimate nature of existence.

Conclusion

This glossary of terms related to Yogamaya and Hindu philosophy provides a foundation for understanding the rich tapestry of ideas and teachings explored in this journey. Each term is a doorway to deeper exploration, inviting readers to reflect on their meanings and implications in the context of their own spiritual journeys.

As you continue to immerse yourself in these teachings, consider revisiting this glossary as a reference. Let each term resonate within you, inspiring curiosity and inquiry. The language of Yogamaya and Hindu philosophy is not merely academic; it is a living expression of the spiritual quest, guiding seekers toward greater awareness, connection, and liberation. In this ever-unfolding journey, may you find the wisdom and understanding that illuminates your path, revealing the profound truths that lie beyond the illusions of existence.

Printed in Great Britain
by Amazon